Plato

Jesus

Rousseau

Schopenhauer

Proudhon

L eo Nikolayevitch Tolstoy, born in 1828 of an ancient Russian noble family, saw active duty as an officer in the Crimean War. In 1861, after two journeys abroad, he finally settled down on the family estate at Yasnaya Polyana. Here his two chief works, *War and Peace* (1864-1868) and *Anna Karenina* (1873-1877), were written. About 1880 he began to devote himself to religious and ethical questions, and thus came into conflict with every kind of authority. Some of his writings were prohibited by the government, and he himself was excommunicated from the Church by the Holy Synod. In his 83rd year, he fled from his own house, not sure where he was going, to die lonely at the remote railway station Astapovo.

# LEO TOLSTOY

Мой отец говорил: Вера дает душевный мир; сознание безсмерт[?]
вечности души дает могущество.
Эти его слова мне всегда помогали в жизни. И сейчас мне - что
они помогли...когда они примерзли в бегу по льду.
Поклонись Его могиле.
Спасибо! Александра Толстая (92 года). 18 дек.
1977

# Michael Levin takes in–depth look at life of Leo Tolstoy

This is an unusual and insightful book focusing on the highlights of Leo Tolstoy's thought and values.

This book is personal and touching in a manner few books are written these days.

The main objective in producing "A Signature on a Portrait" was to remind people about the highly humanitarian ideas of a great writer and a philosopher that he himself has come to love and revere.

> Don Denevi
> San Francisco, California

We have found this book most interesting and enlightening, as it express so well Leo Tolstoy's highly humanitarian ideals, so much ahead of his time.

> Nathalie F. Seitzew
> Social Conselor
> Tolstoy Foundation
> São Paulo, Brazil

Leo Tolstoy with daughter Alexandra

L.N Tolstoy, Moscow, 1868
Photograph taken during the writing of
"War and Peace".

# A SIGNATURE ON
# A
# PORTRAIT

# A SIGNATURE ON
# A
# PORTRAIT

## HIGHLIGHTS OF TOLSTOY'S
## THOUGHT

Third Edition

**Presented By**
**Michael L. Levin**

**The Levin Press**

**New York**                    **Moscow**

**Yasnaya Polyana**

A Signature on a Portrait
Highlights of Tolstoy's Thought
© by The Levin Press


Third Edition


Library of Congress Catalog Card
Number: 90-92256

ISBN 978-0-962-84734-8 (Hardcover)
ISBN 978-0-962-84735-6 (Paperback)

Printed in the United States of America
at Patsons Press, Sunnyvale California

Published by The Levin Press
Tel: (650)968-0660
E-mail:thelevinpress@comcast.net
http://hometown.aol.com/thelevinpress

The author would like to thank John Hessler at Patsons Press
for editorial services, Raj Kumar at Abby Photo for restoration
and developing of the photographs, and his wife Marian for
providing the comfort to write this book.

No one in the West, before Him or since, has written and spoken on non-violence so fully or insistently and with such penetration and insight as He.

Mahatma Gandhi

L. N. Tolstoy, 1854
The happiest time of his life.

The Kingdom of God is within you, and you are to be the pattern after which the Kingdom of this world is to fashion itself.

Young man, you sweat too much blood for the world; sweat some for yourself first. You cannot make the world better till you are better.

Leo Tolstoy

"To read a philosopher's biography, instead of studying his thoughts, is like neglecting a picture and attending only to the style of its frame, debating whether it is carved well or ill, and how much it cost to gild it... Great minds, of which there is scarcely one in a hundred millions, are thus the lighthouses of humanity, and without them mankind would lose itself in the boundless sea of monstrous error and bewilderment..."

– Arthur Schopenhauer, "On Genius"

"The happiest man is the one who
can connect the end of his life with its
beginning"

Goethe

# Contents

|  | Page |
|---|---|
| Preface | 1 |
| Alexandra Tolstoy in her last Year | 5 |
| Tolstoy's philosophy | 11 |
| Excerpts from reminiscences of Tolstoy and analyses of his work by other writers | 17 |
| Tatiana Kuzminskaia | 17 |
| Valentin Bulgakov | 18 |
| Sergei Tolstoy | 20 |
| Alexandra Tolstoy | 21 |
| Ernest Crosby | 23 |
| Dimitri Merejkowski | 28 |
| Vladimir Chertkov | 30 |
| Romain Rolland | 31 |
| Stefan Zweig | 33 |
| Ernest Simmons | 35 |
| Aylmer Maude | 38 |
| Nathan Dole | 42 |
| Edward Steiner | 44 |
| Lectures on Tolstoy | 83 |
| Highlights of Tolstoy's life | 95 |
| The Tolstoy Family | 99 |

A visit to Alexandra Tolstoy                101
Funeral of Alexandra Tolstoy               113
Conclusion                                 121
"What Men live by"                         139
Bibliography                               191
Tolstoy Museum                             195
Illistrations                              197

# PREFACE

After personal knowledge of and careful research about Tolstoy and his family, we believe that however long ago the great writer lived, he has profound meaning and instructional value for the world at large.

Scholars exist everywhere who want to seem very learned and sophisticated because they love and admire the far-off Tolstoy. We have found through personal experience that what people can love about Tolstoy and what gets through to them is neither far off nor sophisticated. It is today; it is highly humanitarian and it is what gives them the glow when they hear his ideas.

We have spent the last eight years doing research on Tolstoy, visiting the Tolstoy Foundation in Valley Cottage, New York, searching through first editions and works of other scholars, and we have developed a visual, music-filled, thought-provoking lecture which persons in and around Connecticut, New York City and Northern California have heard more than two dozen times.

Tolstoy is almost always associated with those difficult Russian names from *Anna Karenina* and *War and Peace*, and almost always viewed as an author of realism, instead of love. This is not the Tolstoy we have come to know. In this short essay, we hope to honor Tolstoy for what we have found him to be: a great, highly unrecognized humanitarian-philosopher who has much relevance to today.

His influence on American literature is largely unknown. In the book *Editor of Genius* by Scott Berg we found that Maxwell E. Perkins, the greatest editor in American history, an employee of Scribner's Book Company, recommended to F. Scott Fitzgerald, Ernest Hemingway and Thomas Wolfe to read *War and Peace*, to read Tolstoy and to study his style. He gave each a copy when he met them. Each, it was written later, thought it was something personal.

But actually, it was something standard for Maxwell Perkins. So, these great American geniuses were asked to raise their level of quality up to Tolstoy's. And, of course, Perkins edited their work with the Tolstoy style in mind. Thus, a great deal of United States literature was profoundly affected by Tolstoy.

The author of this book is Russian by birth and he often traveled with tourists to Yasnaya Polyana, Tolstoy's ancestral home; therefore he is in possession of first-hand knowledge of Tolstoy's real home and values. Tolstoy's lifestyle and history are familiar to us.

So, when we have come upon a man so kind and so understanding of the young and the poor, of sinner and saint, and we see him in the context of his almost princely status, we truly realize his value as a human being and how he should be seen.

And so, we tried to put forth some of the rare and touching things which we have gathered together about Tolstoy. And we also offer some new ideas which we have developed after many years of research.

## ALEXANDRA TOLSTOY IN HER
## LAST YEAR

Alexandra Tolstoy became important in my life when I met Michael for the first time -- June 19, 1978. He had met her when he took to her a picture of Tolstoy to autograph. The inscription she wrote shall stand in history and we will treasure and display it in our home always.

After I became so interested in her life and times, Michael asked me to go to the Tolstoy Foundation for a visit. What a wonderful day! For the first time, I met Tatiana Schaufuss, the lifelong friend of Miss Tolstoy. She reflected on her 90 years with a deep inner strength.

The Tolstoy Foundation is a wonderful place founded 40 years ago at Valley Cottage, New York, which later became a nursing home. On the more than 70 acres are a beautiful Russian Orthodox church, an old swimming pool, grape vines, cottages, a main house, another house where Miss Schaufuss took care of Miss Tolstoy, and the sprawling modern nursing home with hundreds of beds. Finally, there is the Tolstoy Museum complete with a live-in curator. What can be seen and learned is immense.

Every artifact has a relation to Leo Tolstoy, Miss Alexandra Tolstoy or Miss Schaufuss. Their time of friendship and achievement goes back to or before the 20th century, and their nursing skills brought them the highest honors on many battlefields where Russians fought. These two women were friends who never separated.

We saw Miss Tolstoy in a hospital-style bedroom, which Miss Schaufuss tried to make as homelike as possible. Yet, in September 1978, Alexandra was bedridden, but extremely lucid and anxious to talk in both Russian and English. And talk we did! Miss Tolstoy spoke of Russia, her father, and the old days. I began to cry when I thought of her value - her life at Yasnaya Polyana, years before, when she was secretary to the greatest writer who had ever lived.

Could we find questions for a woman who had lived 94 years? We began to speak with her and no questions were needed.

She reflected on Russia from days past when Miss Tolstoy was young. She wanted to be in her old home again, picking mushrooms with her father, but, would the Russians want her home? She said, "They would kill me." What then was expressed about Tolstoy's writing was amazing. "Tolstoy didn't care as much for *War and Peace* " she said. He preferred a small story, "What Men Live By." Peasants, he felt, were more interesting than any other people. The more we spoke with her, the more I realized that Konstantin Levin, the man in *Anna Karenina* who left society to go to the country, was Tolstoy.

Miss Tolstoy spoke English beautifully and she made me very proud to be marrying a Russian. Twenty minutes passed, and obviously our presence tired her, so Miss Schaufuss invited us for tea and discussion. The beauty of their lives became clearer to me. One year later it was sad to be at the Tolstoy Foundation for the second time, for Alexandra Tolstoy's funeral.

It was, for me, a dreamlike time. The rain, heavy at times did not seem an annoyance. It came and went - and although the mud was becoming wetter and deeper, it only added to the beauty and tragedy of it all. The wet blades of grass were like stars evoking to me thoughts of what Russia once had been, of Czars and the great palaces of these old people and their grandchildren -- how far away they all were. Inside the small Russian Orthodox church, the flowers represented respect to a now almost-smiling Miss Tolstoy.

The mass, three hours long, was also of a time gone by. A reporter came all the way from the West Coast and pictures were taken. Unfortunately, Miss Tolstoy was driven to an Orthodox graveyard, miles away from the Tolstoy Foundation to be buried; she should have been buried with her father in Yasnaya Polyana.

Many thoughts have passed through my head. So beautiful a place as Valley Cottage, above Nyack, is not well known since Miss Tolstoy herself did not get the recognition that she deserved from the American people. She was the last of an era, the daughter of a pure genius. No one of importance was at the funeral and no one of importance said anything. Already as I write this, she is forgotten. Shall it be said that in forgetting, or not caring for our deepest values, we are ultimately harming ourselves?

The Hemingways and the Fitzgeralds are always just a phrase away when we speak of novels, but the daughter of the greatest was truly ignored. Her knowledge could have helped us to be wiser, stronger, and closer to a mind never to come again.

In my heart is warmth for those who continue to cherish the fine spirit of the Tolstoy name, and I respect Michael Levin for being strong and clear enough to appreciate a light now extinguished. For a little while, that light bathed us with inspiration.

Nancy J. Levin, Written October 1, 1979
First anniversary of the death of Alexandra Tolstoy

## TOLSTOY'S PHILOSOPHY

For many, Tolstoy's philosophy is epitomized in the "five commandments" which he drew from the teachings of Christ:

1. Do not be angry.
2. Do not commit adultery.
3. Do not bind yourself to oaths.
4. Do not defend yourself with violence.
5. Do not go to war.

He felt these held the answer to the question: "What is the meaning of life?", a question that troubled him for so long and which finally brought about a spiritual crisis.

In 1883 he explained himself at greater length in the essay "What I believe." "Since all know that the meaning of Christ's teaching is based on love to man," he declared then "resist not him that is evil, means... never do an act of violence, an act contrary to love, whatever the insult or harm you may bear."

He imagined the whole of Christendom rearing the young according to the "five commandments" rather than regular church attendance, prayers, abstinence from meat on Friday, and fasting every Lent. Fulfillment of Christ's teaching is expressed in his commandments and efforts at establishing the Kingdom of God on earth which could bring the highest blessing attainable by man–peace.

"People always say that strict observance of Christ's teachings would surely bring about the Kingdom of God on earth," he wrote, "but since observance is impossibly difficult, the teaching is impracticable."

"What are the chief conditions of indisputable happiness? One is man's union with nature. The others are work which one is fond of and is voluntary, physical labor which gives one an appetite, and sound sleep is another condition of happiness."

Christ simply asks us not to torment ourselves by following the World's false teaching – Christ does not call upon us to make sacrifices, but only to do what is better for us here in this life. If men live without property and resisting others, Christ teaches, then they will be happier.

"[It was not the Church but the people who] abolished slavery, which the Church justified – religious executions, the power (sometimes by the Church) of Emperors and Popes, and the people have now begun to ask what will come in the next turn: the abolition of property and the state [in part, a rather striking prophetic insight on the Russian Revolution, which occurred 33 years later]."

Tolstoy calls for a rebirth of the Church in the spirit of Christ's teachings as he understands them. If you consider it irrational to kill people in war, to benefit from the labor of the poor, to imprison men, to live in the polluted atmosphere of cities, then he calls upon all to avoid these things.

Once he understood the meaning of Christ's revelation "the truth will set you free," he felt free himself, completely free.

The change that would improve the world, he believed, had to come from within. In *The Law of Love and the Law of Violence* (1909) he wrote:

"All thinking people must admit that the present life of Christian nations will deteriorate more and more if we cannot make up our minds to modify it. The misery of the disinherited and the luxury of the rich increase each day; the struggle of all against all; revolutionaries against governments, governments against revolutionaries, oppressed nations against their oppressors, state against state, the West against the East it is becoming even more bitter..."

... Each step that we may take towards material progress not only fails to advance us towards the general well-being but shows on the contrary, that all these technical improvements increase our misery. Submarines, subterranean aerial machines may be invented for transporting men with the rapidity of lightning; the means of communicating speech and human thought may be multiplied ad infinitum; but it would still remain a fact that the travellers who are so comfortably and rapidly transported, are neither willing nor able to commit anything but evil, and their thoughts and words can only incite men to further harm.

"People who are against the present system (regime) and government try to destroy them by using violent methods. But what is the difference if instead of Nicolas II there will be Petrunkevitch?"

K. B. wrote that it is most important that people themselves have to become better so their life would be happier. For this, people have to pay more attention to their inner, spiritual life.

## EXCERPTS FROM REMINISCENCES OF TOLSTOY AND ANALYSES OF HIS WORKS BY OTHER WRITERS WHICH HELPED ILLUMINATE HIS THINKING

From the book MY LIFE AT HOME AND IN YASNAYA POLYANA by Tatiana Kuzminskaia (1846-1925), sister-in-law of Tolstoy, the youngest sister of S. A. Tolstoy

In his youth, L. N. Tolstoy suffered because he was not satisfied with his appearance. Later on, when his children grew up, if we started to judge somebody, he would tell us with a smile: "Don't judge, so you won't be judged." Once for a joke, I responded: "But this is so much fun."

"Yes, I know, lots of times you feel like teasing. I, for instance, would never do this, etc. Especially this, is characteristic to women." But he left the room because of the women's protests.

From the book THE LAST YEAR OF LEO
TOLSTOY by Valentin Bulgakov (1886-). He was
employed as secretary to Tolstoy in 1910. Bulgakov
offers many instances of the words of the great
writer which provide insight on his ideas.

All the inventions of the civilizations are
convenient and interesting just at the beginning
- later people get bored with them. For example,
the phonograph (Thomas Edison gave Tolstoy a
phonograph as a present). This is simply terrible.

[In a conversation about the upbringing of
children, he stated the following:] There is no
need for education. Indeed, this is not a paradox,
as it is said about me, but my conviction that the
more educated a person, the more he is ignorant.
For me, the words "educated" and "ignorant" are
synonymous.

Tolstoy said, "I must tell about the whole
civilization the following: Let civilization be lost to
the devil, but for music, I would be sorry."

"There is no way without religion; otherwise the corruption and vodka will be forever."

"I don't believe in any presentiment except in presentiment of death."

Leo Tolstoy gave a very interesting definition of insanity. He said: "I do not agree with the scientists' definition of mental illness – insanity. In my opinion, insanity is the lack of receptivity to other peoples' ideas: An insane person holds with certitude only to what has taken root in his own mind. He will not understand me. There are two kinds of men. One is distinguished by his receptiveness, his sensitivity to the ideas of others. He is in communication with all the wise men of the world – both ancients and those living today. He gathers impressions from everywhere: from them, from his childhood, what his nurse told him ... and the other kind of man knows only what occurred to his mind only..."

From the book NOTES OF THE PAST
by Sergei Tolstoy (1863–1947), son of Tolstoy

[Tolstoy tried to understand why music so strongly affects the feelings. His son quotes him:] "Music doesn't give effect on my mind or imagination. When I listen to music, I don't think of anything and I don't imagine anything, but somewhere deep in my soul, my soul gets filled with an unusually delightful feeling to such an extent that I am losing the awareness of my existence and this feeling is remembrance. But the remembrance of what? Although the sensation is very strong, it is unclear. It seems that you recall something which never indeed happened. If we pretend that the music is – a remembrance of feelings – then it will become clear why it gives different effects for different people. The more pure and happy is the past of a person, the more he enjoys the music. But, on the contrary, the more difficult the past was, the less joy the music brings. That is why some people cannot stand music.

From the book TOLSTOY: A LIFE OF MY
FATHER
by Alexandra Tolstoy (1884-1974), his youngest
daughter

[As a child, Tolstoy's eldest brother, Nikolai, used
to make up imaginative tales about the Moravian
Brethren, a religious group which functioned in
the area and whose ideal of love remained with the
writer all his life. Alexandra Tolstoy recounts how in
later years her father used to refer to one of Nikolai's
tales:] "Their principal secret of what to do so that
nobody would have any more unhappiness, nor
ever quarrel, and always would be happy — that
was inscribed on a green stick, and this stick was
buried near the rim of the ravine in the old Zakaz
Forest, and in the same place, since my body must
be buried somewhere, I have asked in memory of
Nikolenka that I can be laid to rest."

[Music always exercised a powerful influence
over Tolstoy. Mozart, Haydn, Schubert, Chopin were
his favorite composers. Yet his love for classical music
did not, in any way interfere with his fondness for
folk and gypsy music.] Music was to him a divine

manifestation of the human soul.

[In February 1870, Tolstoy made the first outline of *Anna Karenina*.] Dostoyevsky wrote: "Anna Karenina, as a masterpiece, is perfection. Nothing in the literature of Europe, at the present time, compares with it.

Before his death, Tolstoy wrote: "God is the infinite All: Man is only a finite manifestation.... God is what truly exists. Man is his manifestation in matter, time and space. The more the manifestation of God in man (life), unites itself with manifestations (the lives) of other beings, the more he himself exists. The union of his life with the lives of other beings, is accomplished through love.

"God is not love, but the more love man has, the more he manifests God, the more he truly exists."

From the book TOLSTOY AS A
SCHOOLMASTER
by Ernest Crosby (1856-1906), American Tolstoy
scholar who met him in Yasnaya Polyana

In a short article printed as a leaflet by the Free
Age Press, London (Free Age Press Leaflet, No. 4),
Tolstoy lays down the rules which, in his opinion,
should govern a religious education:

If I know how to transmit to a child the substance
of the religious teaching I consider this to be the
truth, he says. I should say to him that we have come
into this world and live in it, not according to our
own will, but according to the will of that which we
call God, and it will therefore be well with us only
when we fulfill this will. This will is that we should
all be happy; and for all to be happy, there is but one
means: each must act towards others as he would
wish that they should act towards him.

"As to the questions about how the world
came into existence, and what awaits us after death,
I would answer the first by the acknowledgement

of my ignorance and of the anomaly of such a question (in all of the Buddhist world, no such question exists); and the second, I would answer by the conjecture that the will of Him who called us into life for our welfare leads us somewhere through death -probably for the same purpose."

From the book TOLSTOY AND HIS MESSAGE by Ernest Crosby

Do we ask if Christ draws a sharp line between rich and poor? There is nothing more deadening to true life than wealth and purpose and fine linen and the accompanying pride. We can, each of us, test the truth for ourselves. There is, on a Sunday morning, in any of our East Side Catholic churches in New York, a Christian feeling of communion and communism which is not to be found in fashionable congregations. Is it possible to feel the brotherhood of man in East Broadway or Hester Street as it cannot be felt on Fifth Avenue?

William Lloyd Garrison was a non-resistant and one of the most extreme. Is it a mere coincidence that this typical non-resistant should have been the man who, in the history of America, has, without any exception, accomplished the most for humanity? At the close of the war, when President Lincoln was congratulated on having liberated the slaves, he replied with much truth, that he had been an instrument and that the moral power of Garrison and his followers had done all. I must dwell for a moment upon the character of Garrison to show what stuff non-resistants are made of.

Let us judge him by the first number of *The Liberation*, which was published on January 1, 1831. Garrison had just been released from jail, a penniless youth of five and twenty, without resources or connections. He bought some paper and second-hand type on credit; he and his assistant were forced by want to live for many months chiefly on "bread and milk", when they both slept on the floor. From this point of vantage he thundered forth in his first leading article:

"The standard is now unfurled ... Let the enemies of the persecuted blacks tremble. I will be as harsh as Truth and as uncompromising as Justice ... I am in earnest. I will not equivocate; I will not excuse; I will not retract a single inch; and I WILL BE HEARD. Posterity will bear testimony that I was right." And posterity has so borne witness and has long since decided that no man ever did a man's work in a manlier way than the non-resistant Garrison.

Another interesting example of non-resistance is given in King's *History of Ohio*. He devotes one chapter to the Moravians who in the eighteenth century went into the wilderness to preach this doctrine to the savages. Here are King's words:"The faith they sought to implant was manly love. To go in this panoply before the wild Indians of America, it must be admitted, was proof of great faith."

It would be a mistake to consider Tolstoy's views as the product of an isolated mind. He is, in many respects, the representation of all that is best in his dearly beloved Russian peasantry. Leroy Beaulieu tells us in his works on the *Empire of the Tsars and the Russians* (Vol. III, Chap. 3), that the Russian common people are remarkable for their "charity and humility, and what is rarer still and almost unknown in the same class in other countries, for their spirit of asceticism and renouncement, love of poverty, and the taste for self-mortification and sacrifice." He also shows us that the moral ideal of the people is complete chastity. It is then as the mouthpiece of the Russian peasantry, among whom he has learned the lessons of his life, that Tolstoy finds his chief significance and they are fortunate in having a man of such genius and character to represent them. Great teacher-peasant nobleman, this aristocrat, born into the ruling class of an autocracy, who condemns all government and caste, this veteran of two wars who proscribes all bloodshed, this keen sportsman turned vegetarian, this landlord who follows Henry George, this man of wealth who will have nothing to do with money, this famous novelist who thinks that he wasted his time in writing most of his novels, this rigid moralist, one of whose books, at least, *The Kreutzer Sonata,* was banned by the American Post Office. That same dramatic instinct, which made him a great novelist, which impelled Sir Henry Irving to rank his two plays among the best of the past century, and which, as we have seen, has so often led him to find lessons in the active world around him, this same instinct has made this least theatrical and most self-forgetful of men the dramatic pre-figuration in his own person of a reunited race, set free by love from the shackles of caste and violence. As it was with the prophets of old, so with him, there is a deeper significance in his life in the tragedy of himself, than in the burden of his spoken message. He is the protagonist today of the drama of the human soul. A stage which can put forward such a protagonist has no reason for despair.

From the book TOLSTOY AS MAN AND ARTIST
by Dimitri Merejkowski (1865-1941), Tolstoy Scholar

"What is the meaning of getting on in years?" asks Tolstoy in 1894. "It means that your hair is coming out, your teeth are decaying, wrinkles are coming and your breath is unpleasant ... Where is that of which I was the servant? Where has beauty gone? All is gone; nothing is left, life is over."

Tolstoy and Dostoyevysky are the two great columns, standing apart in the propylaeum of the temple - parts facing each other, set over against each other in the edifice, incomplete and still obscured by scaffolding, that temple of Russian religion which will be, I believe, the future religion of the whole world.

"When did I begin to be?" says Tolstoy, in the fragment "Earliest Recollections." "When did my life commence? Did I not live when I learned to see, to hear, to understand, to speak; when I slept and drank, and kissed the breast and laughed, and delighted my mother? Yes, I lived, and lived happily."

"Did I not then acquire so much, so quickly, that all the rest of my life, I have not acquired a hundredth part of the same? From the five-year old child to me, there is but a step. Between the embryo and the newborn is a gulf. And between the non-existent and the embryo lies far, far more a distance utterly inaccessible to our conceptions."

From the book THE LAST DAYS OF TOLSTOY
by V. G. Chertkov (1854-1936), closest friend of Leo
Tolstoy

[From a letter by Tolstoy] April 14, 1910. You ask
whether I like the life in which I find myself. No I
don't like it. I don't like it because I am living with
my own people in luxury while there is poverty
and want around me, and I cannot get away from
the luxury and I cannot help the poverty and want.
For this, I do not like my life. I like it in that it is
in my power to act, and that I can act, and that I
do act in the measure of my strength in accordance
with the teachings of Christ, to love God and my
neighbor. To love God means to love the perfection
of goodness and to approach it as far as one can. To
love one's neighbor is to love all people alike as one's
brothers and sisters. It is this, and this alone, that I
am striving for, and since, little by little, however
poorly I am approaching it, I do not grieve but only
rejoice. You ask me too, if I rejoice, at I what rejoice,
and what joy do I expect? I rejoice that I can carry
out to the measure of my strength, the task set me

by my Master; to work for the setting up of that
Kingdom of God to which we are all striving.

From the book TOLSTOY
by Romain Rolland (1866-1944), a famous French
writer

The cornerstone of his philosophy is the Sermon
on the Mount, whose teachings Tolstoy expresses in
five commandments:

1. Do not be angry.
2. Do not commit adultery.
3. Do not take oaths.
4. Do not resist evil by evil.
5. Be no man's enemy.

This is the negative part of the doctrine;
the positive portion is contained in this single
commandment:

Love God, and thy neighbor as thyself.

And Tolstoy adds naively:

"Strange as it may seem, I have been obliged,
after eighteen centuries, to discover these rules as a
novelty."

"Love is the only reasonable activity of man; love is the most reasonable and most enlightened state of the soul."

"I believe that this increase of love will contribute, more than any other factor, to founding the kingdom of God upon earth."

"The pivot of the evil is property. Property is merely the means of enjoying the labor of others."

Although Resurrection has not the harmonious fullness of the work of his youth, and although I, for my part, prefer *War and Peace*, it is nonetheless one of the most beautiful poems of human compassion; perhaps the most truthful ever written.

[Rolland quotes Tolstoy's words:] "The greatest modern sin: the abstract love of humanity, impersonal love for those who are somewhere out of sight. To love those we do not know, those whom we shall never meet, is so easy a thing! There is no need to sacrifice anything; and at the same time, we are so pleased with ourselves! The conscience is fooled.

No, we must love our neighbors, those we live with and who are, in our way, an embarrassment to us."

From the book THE LIVING THOUGHTS OF TOLSTOY
by Stefan Zweig, a famous German writer

[On a sheet of paper he listed the six unknown questions which he had to answer:]

1. What is the cause for my existence and that of everyone else?
2. Why am I living?
3. What purpose has my existence or any other?
4. What does the division which I feel within me into good and evil signify and for what purpose is it there?
5. How must I live?
6. What is death – how can I save myself?

[At another time he said:] :"The Church knows that anyone who means to shape his life according to the letter of the Bible is bound to come in conflict with the official standard of the Church and the laws of the state."

The Church authorities had to excommunicate Tolstoy. For Tolstoy, stirred to his depths of being, began to undermine all the foundations of church, state and temporal order.

Tolstoy was now unavoidably on the way to becoming the most determined enemy of the state, the most passionate anarchist and anti-collectivist of modern times... No one was a more effective destructive critic of society than the man who had been the greatest artistic creator of his epoch.

[He also attacked private property:] "Today possessions are the root of all evil. They cause the suffering of those who possess and those who do not possess."

What Tolstoy dreams of... is revolution, from within, revolution not of the mailed fist, but of a conscience unshakable and ready for any suffering - a revolution of souls, not fists.

From the book LEO TOLSTOY

by Ernest J. Simmons, biographer of Tolstoy, formerly professor of Russian literature in Columbia University, internationally recognized Tolstoy scholar

A Western critic once remarked that if life could write, it would write just as Tolstoy did.

[Simmons quotes critic N. N. Strakhov as saying that Tolstoy presented] "complete picture of human life. A complete picture of the Russia of that day. A complete picture of what may be called the history and struggles of people. A complete picture of everything in which people find their happiness and greatness, their grief and humiliation. That is "*War and Peace.*"

From the book INTRODUCTION TO TOLSTOY'S WRITINGS
by Ernest J. Simmons, Tolstoy's Biographer and Scholar

[Simmons quotes Tolstoy as saying:] "The Kingdom of God on earth can be achieved by everyone first realizing that the Kingdom was within himself."

As examples of this highest art "flowing from love of God and Man" in literature, Tolstoy mentioned Schiller's *The Robbers;*
Hugo's *Les Miserables and Les Pauvres Gens;*
Dickens's *A Tale of Two Cities, A Christmas Carol, The Chimes, David Copperfield* and *Pickwick Papers;*
Harriet Beecher Stowe's *Uncle Tom's Cabin;*
Dostoevsky's *The House of the Dead;*
George Eliot's *Adam Bede;*
Cervantes' *Don Quixote;*
Moliere's Comedies; *Tales of Pushkin and Gogol."*

Tolstoy wrote, "Some people who are together, if not hostile to one another, are at least estranged in mood and feelings, till perhaps a story, a performance, a picture or even a building, but more often of all, music, unites them all as by an electric flash, and in place of their former isolation or even enmity, they are conscious of union and mutual love. Each is glad that the other feels what he feels, glad of the communion established not only between him and all present...And this effect is produced both by religious art which transmits feelings of love of God and one's neighbor, and by universal art transmitting the very simplest feelings common to all men."

When an American newspaper asked Tolstoy in 1899 to comment on a proposal of the Tsar for a "summit conference" of the great powers at the Hague, to consider the question of disarmament in the interest of world peace, he replied: "My answer to your question is that peace can never be achieved by conferences or be decided by people who not only jabber, but who themselves go to war... All such conferences can be summed up in a single dictum: All people are sons of God and brothers, and therefore, they ought to love and not kill each other. Forgive my sharpness, but these conferences invoked in me a strong feeling of disgust over the hypocrisy that is so obvious in them."

*The Kreutzer Sonata* caused more immediate public furor than any of Tolstoy's published works... Priests gave sermons denouncing Tolstoy; a high government official urged the emperor to punish him; and the work was banned in mails by the United States postal authorities.

From the book LEO TOLSTOY
by Aylmer Maude (1858-1938), biographer and scholar of Tolstoy

[Maude quotes Tolstoy:] "The powerful means to true happiness in life, is like a spider, to let flow from oneself on all sides of a cobweb of love, and to catch in it all that comes to hand: women, old or young, children, or policemen."

No bad weather was allowed to interfere with his daily walk. He could put up with loss of appetite, but he could never go a day without a brisk walk in the open air. If his literary work went badly, or if he wished to throw off the effects of any unpleasantness, a long walk was his sovereign remedy. He could walk a whole day without fatigue, and we have frequently ridden together for ten or twelve hours.

All luxury was distasteful to him; and such that ordinary people regard as common conveniences seemed to him harmful indulgence, bad for the souls and bodies of men.

In contrast to his former habit, he dressed very simply, and when at home, never wore starched shirts or tailor-made clothes, but adapted to his own requirements the ordinary Russian blouse, as was at that time a not uncommon practice among Russian country gentlemen. His outdoor winter dress was also an adaptation of the peasant's coat and sheepskin overcoat.

Sometimes he would ironically remark that, though he had not earned a Generalship in the artillery, he had, at any rate, won his Generalship in literature.

[Tolstoy wrote:] "I reject neither real life, nor the labor necessary for its maintenance; but it seems to me that the greater part of my life and yours is taken up with satisfying not our natural wants, but wants invented by us or artificially inoculated by our education and habitual to us; and that nine-tenths of the work we devote to satisfying those demands, is idle work. I should very much like to be firmly convinced that I give people more than I take from them; but as I feel myself much disposed to value my own work high and other people's work low, I do not hope by simply intensifying my labor and choosing what is most difficult, to assure myself that their account with me does not land them in a loss. (I am sure to tell myself that the work I like is the most necessary and difficult). Therefore, I wish to take as little from others as possible, and to work as much as possible for the satisfaction of my own needs; and I think that is the easiest way to avoid making a mistake."

Tolstoy did not, at this time, foresee one very important consequence of the task he had set himself. The Russians were then still generally devoted to "the Tsar, the Faith and Fatherland." That trinity was interdependent. The Tsar appointed the Head of the Holy Synod, whose duty it was to see that the Church upheld the Throne. The Tsars had always been the center to which the nation rallied for defense against foreign foes. It was important for Russia to be defeated without the Tsar's prestige suffering, or for the Tsar to be discredited without the fabric of the Empire being endangered. It followed (though it was several years before Tolstoy denounced patriotism, and still longer before he denounced the Tsar) that from the moment he attacked the Church, he laid his ax to the root of a tree that was of enormous importance to the whole social edifice, and prepared the ground for a Revolution, which when it came, took forms he would have found abhorrent.

At this time, he wrote, *What Men Live By* (in twenty-three tales), the precursor of a long series of admirably simple and beautiful stories intended primarily for peasants and children, but which have become popular among all classes and in all languages. Of these, Carmen Sylva, the late Queen of Rumania wrote:"Of all the works this great man and artist has written, his short stories have made the strongest impression upon me. I regard them as the most perfect tales ever written. In these popular stories, thought of the highest purity reaches us, which to my mind is far more eloquent than the subtlest style... It surprises me that people speak more of the so-called greater works of Tolstoy than of these little gems, which are quite unique. If he had written nothing but these short stories, he would still rank among the greatest men of the world."

From the book NOTES FROM THE LIFE OF TOLSTOY
by N. H. Dole, biographer of Tolstoy

[Dole quotes Tolstoy:] "A conversation about religion and faith suggested to me a great, stupendous idea, to the realization of which I feel that I am capable of devoting my life. This idea is to establish a new religion suited to the present state of mankind – the religion of Jesus but purified from dogma and mysticism, a practical religion, not promising future bliss, but giving bliss on earth. I realize that this can be accomplished only by generations consciously working toward it. One generation will hand on the idea to the next and, some day, enthusiasm or reason will accomplish it. Deliberately to promote the union of mankind by means of religion is the basic principle of the idea, which I hope will command my enthusiasm."

[Dole also quotes Maude's, *The Life of Tolstoy*:] "His genius, sincerity, industry, courage, endurance and tenacity; his marvelous intuition, extraordinary capacity for observation and artistic reproduction; his devotion to the service of truth and goodness; his self-abnegation, his concentration upon the most vital branches of human thought, and his feeling attractive, mark him, by far, as the greatest and most interesting man alive."

[Dole also offers a quote from W. T. Stead:] "In Russia and out of Russia, I have found people more interested in the personality of Count Leo Tolstoy, the novelist, than in that of any other living Russian. He is the first man of letters in contemporary Russia, but that alone would not account for the wide-spread interest in his character. He is a great original, an independent thinker, a religious teacher and the founder of something that is midway between a church, a school and a socio-political organization. He not only thinks strange things and says them with rugged force and vivid utterance -he does strange things, and, what is more, he induces others to do the same. A man of genius who spends his time planting potatoes and cobbling shoes, a great literary artist who founded a propaganda of Christian anarchy, an aristocrat who spends his life as a peasant - such a man in any country would command attention. In Russia, he monopolizes it."

From the book TOLSTOY, THE MAN AND HIS MESSAGE
by Dr. Edward A. Steiner, professor of Applied Christianity in Iowa college

[At the end of the nineteenth century, Steiner occupied the professorship of Applied Christianity in Iowa College, and spent several months in Russia at the request of the Outlook Company and under its commission for the express purpose of obtaining material for his book. Dr. Steiner not only had the opportunity to discuss with the great Russian writer and teacher his life and work, he also brought to his task study and appreciation of Tolstoy's character and theories extending over a long period of time.]

A most interesting fact, Tolstoy, like a new Messiah, drew to himself a large number of thinking Jews, some of whom organized communities according to his principles. One of these is Mr. Femerman and another, Mr. Butkyevitch, in the district of Cherson, in southern Russia. Others, emulating Tolstoy's example, forsook their bartering to begin tilling the soil; and the best example is a Jewish colony in Palestine which recruited Jewish university students of Odessa and Moscow, who were "Tolstoy made", as they expressed it. The Jews came to Yasnaya Polyana in goodly numbers to see a man who was really living the Christian life, not merely preaching it. As it is, he has been the Russian who has interpreted Christianity to the Jew in terms which he could accept, and in a form that has nothing to do with idolatry of the Greek Church, which is the greatest barrier to the Jew's acceptance of the Christian religion.

Some people have been repelled by him, but they were those who went to him as they might have gone to pyramids, the battlefield of Waterloo, or to some wonderful freak museum. Rude he never was, although many a time his visitors were as inconsiderate of him as they are of historic places; and only his being very much alive saved him from being carried away bodily by relic hunters.

[Tolstoy told Steiner:] "I do not believe in this new progress it is not a universal law. Progress is not always necessary, nor is it always good. Progress in one direction is paid for by a backward step in another. In Russia, only the useless classes believe in progress; nine-tenths do not believe in it; for it does not add anything to their happiness. The peasant does not need the telegraph, or the railroads which entice him from the country to the city, neither does he need the printing press; he is not quite sure that reading does not spoil him. We must believe the peasants more than we do society; for they are in the majority and without them, society cannot live; but the peasant can live without society."

This is Tolstoy's greatest cry: "The Kingdom of God is within you, and you are to be the pattern after which the Kingdom of this world is to fashion itself." "Young man," he said [to Steiner]. "you sweat too much blood for the world; sweat some for yourself first. You cannot make the world better till you are better."

Tolstoy a man who, like all great prophets, revalued our values, and has proved himself to have been a true essayer of our civilization.

Tolstoy at the University, 1847

Tolstoy in 1856

Sofia Behrs the year before her marriage to Tolstoy, 1861

Tolstoy at the time of his marriage,
October 5, 1862

Sisters Sofia Tolstoy and Tatyana Behrs, 1862.
Sofia Tolstoy at left. Tatyana Behrs was prototype of Natasha
Rostova in *War and Peace*.

Tolstoy in 1876

Tolstoy in 1881

Countess Sophie Andreyevna Tolstoy
in 1881

.Л. Н. Толстой. 1885 г.

Tolstoy in 1885

L.N. Tolstoy in 1887
Portrait by I. Repin

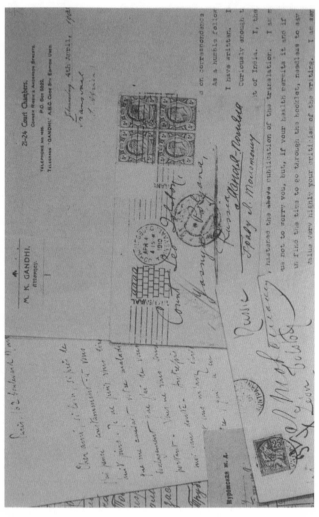

M.K. Gandhi's letter to Tolstoy.
Dated 4th April 1900.

Tolstoy in his Library

Tolstoy in his study

A tea party

Tolstoy in 1892

Tolstoy in 1908

Tolstoy on a walk

Tolstoy returning from bathing

Tolstoy reading in his family circle

Tolstoy and his wife Sofia in 1910

Tolstoy and his daughter Alexandra

Tolstoy in 1910

Leo Tolstoy
One of his last photographs

A phonograph presented to Leo Tolstoy by Thomas Edison.
Before Tolstoy's death in 1910, Thomas Edison made a special
trip to Moscow to present him with this phonograph and
recorded his voice.

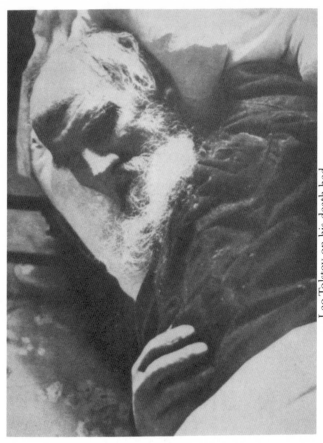

Leo Tolstoy on his death bed
November 7, 1910, Astapovo Station, Russia.

Funeral procession for Tolstoy
November 8, 1910

The Grave of L. N. Tolstoy.
"The plainest grave in the world" –Stefan Zweig.

Michael L. Levin, Winter 1974. Yasnaya Polyana.
It is written on the sign, in Russian:
"To the grave of L. N. Tolstoy"
Photograph by Luba Lazarenko

A picturesque corner of Yasnaya Polyana

In the background is Michael L. Levin with his local friend Luba. Summer 1975.

Michael Levin in front of the Museum of Leo Tolstoy.
Moscow, October 1993.

A view of Yasnaya Polyana in summer. Of his family home Tolstoy said: "I cannot imagine Russia, and my concern for it, without Yasnaya Polyana. Maybe I would be able to see more clearly the common laws that are necessary for the motherland, but I would not love her with such passion."

A view of Yasnaya Polyana, Tolstoy's house, in winter.
Yasnaya Polyana was the place where life and creative literary
and spiritual activity took place, where this genius Russian
writer was born on August 28, 1828, and where he lived and
wrote for almost 60 years. Here, on the edge of a grove of
forest trees, was enough life and recollection to fill so well his
many creative works. In the minds of many visitors, this place
represented a haven where culture, kindness and justice ruled
supreme.

The Chapel of St. Mark's College in Chelsea in London. Tolstoy visited this college in 1861 to study the school system in England.

Author in October 1993 researching Tolstoy's trip to London.
In his hand a book by Victor Lucas: *Tolstoy in London*.

The next pages are credits from various lectures on Tolstoy and his world, as given by Michael Levin.

84

# Library

## East Lyme

Training classes for the Apple II E computer will be conducted Friday, March 16 from 4 to 5 p.m. and Tuesday March 20 from 8 to 9 p.m. at the East Lyme Library.

These classes are for adults and children. Children under nine years of age should be accompanied by an adult. Training is required in order to use the computer. Both training and computer time are free.

A gift from the Friends of the East Lyme Library has made possible the purchas of a printer for the Apple II E computer. Instruction for its use will be given during the training sessions.

* * *

A film series at the library will feature The Ransom of Red Chief and The Little Prince Saturday, March 17 at 1 p.m.

Ransom of Red Chief is based on the famous short story by O. Henry. Two inept con men kidnap the banker's son and hold him for ransom, but young Johnny (Red Chief) drives them to distraction with his antics.

Little Prince is the story of a small boy from another planet who befriends an aviator forced down in the Sahara desert.

* * *

The library's winter film series will present two films for older children Saturday, March 31 at 1 p.m.

A Cricket in Times Square is based on the famous book by Feorge Seldon about living with a music loving family. The Kite Story follows the adventures of a child and a kite on a beautiful spring day.

* * *

These will be the last films in the series.

* * *

The library will sponsor two Apple computer courses Monday thrnngs

from April 2 to 23. Courses will be taught by a certified teacher.

Introduction to Micro Computers for Adults will be conducted from 6:30 to 8 and 8 to 9:30 p.m. Mondays at a cost of $45. Registration is limited. For information call the Reference Department at the library, 739-6926.

* * *

Replicas made of driftwood collected on Connecticut shores by Lou Sternberg, of Niantic are on display the library during the month of March. Reproduced in miniature primitive craft are the old Niantic Seafood and Bait Shop, Highland Light, Cape Cod, Sculpin Gallery, Martha's Vineyard and Brandt Point Lighthouse, Nantucket.

* * *

The library has a number of the most used tax forms. Also Reproducible Federal Tax Forms are available at the reference desk for use

on the photocopy machine. May taxpayers will find this both convenient and time saving.

A set of Tax Information Publications will be found for reference use only. Avalable to be checked out are Your Federal Income Tax (publication 17) and Tax Guide for Small Business (publication 334). Cassettes giving instructions for forms 1040EZ, 1040A, 1040A Schedule 1, 1040: SChedules A, B and W: Special rules for the military and other tax ups may also be checked out for a three week period.

* * *

Featured fiction by Kate Coscarelli is featured at the library in a novel similar to Hollywood Wives and The Debutantes.

Four women who live in California pour out their troubles to each other. All four are struggling for power, security and survival against a background of wealth and glamour. If you

want a light plot and plenty of romance, sign up for this one.

## Waterford

The Quarries of Selden Neck will be the topic of a program to be presented at the Waterford Public Library Thursday, March 15 at 7:30 p.m.

Guest speaker will be David H. Wordell of Salem, who will narrate the history of Selden Neck which lies about a mile south of East Haddam in the Connecticut River. Legends and mysteries surrounding Selden Neck's history abound, according to Wordell, who has spent the last seven years doing research on the area.

The program, sponsored by the Waterford Historical Society and the Connecticut Humanities Council, is free and open to the public. It will be followed by a social hour and

refreshments.

The library will present an illustrated slide lecture on Russian Author Leo Tolstoy Tuesday, March 20 at 7:30 p.m.

Michael I. Levin will be guest lecturer. He is a 1961 MSME graduate of Kalinin Institute in Moscow, U.S.S.R. and has been a professional engineer with a speciality in safety for more than 20 years. An American citizen, Levin emigrated from the U.S.S.R. in 1976. As a part-time excursion guide at the ancestral home of Tolstoy, Yasnaya Polyana, he actively pursued his interest in Tolstoy by learning much about the author and his family.

Levin is currently a Niantic resident and is with Stone and Webster at Millstone III.

A question and answer period will follow the formal presentation. The program is free and open to the

# П. Н. ТОЛСТОЙ
# ВВЕЦЕ́НИЕ

# LEO N. TOLSTOY

L E C T U R E

L E O   T O L S T O Y :
A N   I N T R O D U C T I O N

BY

M I C H A E L   L E V I N

THURSDAY   3:30  P.M.

## april 11th

1 9 8 5

JEROME PARK BRANCH
New York Public Library
118 Eames Place
Bronx, N.Y.   10468
1  212   549-5200

*admission free*

# Л. Н. ТОЛСТОЙ
## ВВЕДЕ́НИЕ

## LEO N. TOLSTOY

L E C T U R E

L E O  T O L S T O Y

AN  INTRODUCTION

BY

M I C H A E L  L E V I N

SATURDAY  2:30 PM

# april 20th

1985

FORT WASHINGTON BRANCH
New York Public Library
535 West 179th Street
New York, N.Y.  10033

1 (212)  927-3533

admission free

# Л. Н. ТОЛСТОЙ
# ВВЕДЕ́НИЕ

# LEO N. TOLSTOY

L E C T U R E
L E O   T O L S T O Y
A N   I N T R O D U C T I O N

BY

M I C H A E L   L E V I N

SATURDAY   2:00 P.M.

april 27th
1985

admission free

# Л. Н. ТОЛСТОЙ
## ВВЕДЕ́НИЕ

# LEO N. TOLSTOY

L E C T U R E
L E O   T O L S T O Y
A N   I N T R O D U C T I O N
BY
M I C H A E L   L E V I N

SATURDAY **may 18**TH
2:00 P.M.
1 9 8 5

INWOOD REGIONAL BRANCH
4790 Broadway
New York, N.Y. 10034
1 (212) 942-2445

*admission free*

**DONNELL LIBRARY CENTER LIBRARY DONNELL**

an illustrated lecture
"TOLSTOY"

Speaker: MICHAEL L. LEVIN

Thursday evening, October 3, 1985 at 6:00 p.m.

Admission free

DONNELL LIBRARY CENTER
20 West 53rd Street

on the mezzanine

621-0618

CAMPBELL PUBLIC LIBRARY
PRESENTS
AN ILLUSTRATED LECTURE
by MICHAEL J. LEVIN

Tolstoy

DISCOVER FASCINATING BITS ABOUT
THIS FAMOUS AUTHOR - AND WHAT
THE CONNECTION IS BETWEEN
TOLSTOY, GANDHI,
AND MARTIN LUTHER KING!

WEDNESDAY FEB. 25, 1987, 7:30 p.m.
CAMPBELL PUBLIC LIBRARY · 77 HARRISON AVE
ADMISSION FREE 378-8122

# Library

## East Lyme

Training classes for the Apple II E computer will be conducted at the East Lyme Public Library Tuesday, April 17 from 9:30 to 10:30 a.m.

There will be a Bank Street Writer demonstration Thursday, April 19 from 9:30 to 10:30 a m. These classes are for adults and children. Children under nine years of age should be accompanied by an adult. Training is required in order to use the computer. Both training and computer time are free.

A gift from the Friends of the Library has made possible the purchase of a printer for the Apple II E computer. Instruction for its use will be given during the training sessions.

••••

Storytelling for children of all ages (and adults also) will be conducted Tuesday, April 17 from 11 a.m. to noon in the Children's Room.

Three Jester Theater Company, a circus of silliness, a trio of trouble, gallons of giggles, masses of mischief, all unfolding as the jesters present an hour of theatrical antics for children of all ages, will be presented Wednesday, April 18 from 10:30 to 11:30 a.m. in St. John's Church across from the library.

••••

There will be a free blood pressure clinic Wednesday, April 25 from 6 to 7 p.m. sponsored by the East Lyme Visiting Nursing Association.

Dr. M. Deren, a thoracic surgeon, will present a film and conduct a question and answer period at 7 p.m., sponsored by the American Cancer Society in conjunction with Cancer Awareness Week.

••••

Mike Caro, a photographer and artist from Niantic, will have his work featured this month in the library's display case.

Caro says his goal in assembling these constructions was to keep the cost extremely low by using only found or available materials, whether from nature, or cast-off manmade objects, today's "new nature."

••••

Featured non-fiction at the library is Collecting American Country by Mary Ellisor Emmerling. The first section contains an alphabetical listing of American Country objects accompanied by a photograph, history, composition and characteristics for each. Following chapters include contemporary craftsmen working in the American mode and advise on how to select, maintain and display country pieces. At the conclusion there are directories to stores offering country pieces, dealers in country antiques, publications for collectors and a guide to experts in preservation and repair.

---

A program on Tolstoy by a former Russian citizen who knew the author's daughter Sasha will be presented at the library Friday, April 27 at 7:30 p.m.

Michael Levin, an engineer at Millstone Point, first started to love Tolstoy as a child in Moscow, where everyone knows and revers the great writer. While studying enginnering at the Kalinin Institute and later working as a safety specialist, Levin used his free time to take people to Tolstoy's ancestral home, Yasnaya Polyana and to his grave. Arriving in the United States in 1976, Levin visited Alexandra Tolstoy, the last living child of the author and remained in close contact with her until her death in 1979, learning much about the life and thought of her father.

In his program Levin will discuss Tolstoy from the perspectives he has gained as a reader, a guide and as a friend of Sasha Tolstoy. He will include slides of Yasnaya Polyana and excerpts by the Russian opera star, Chaliapin.

---

# TOLSTOY

## THE WRITER AND HIS PHILOSOPHY OF NONVIOLENCE

### An Illustrated Lecture by

## MICHAEL LEVIN

*Michael Levin is a native of Moscow, U.S.S.R., who emigrated to the U.S. in 1976. An engineer by profession, he has had a lifelong interest in the great Russian writer Leo Tolstoy. Mr. Levin served as a tour guide at Yasnaya Polyana, the estate where Tolstoy was born, raised his large family, farmed, opened a school for peasant children, and wrote War and Peace and Anna Karenina.*

*Mr. Levin will discuss Tolstoy's life and art and the connection between Tolstoy, Gandhi, and Martin Luther King. The program will include slides of Yasnaya Polyana and a display of important works on Tolstoy.*

**For further information:** 353-2608 or 353-3177 evenings.

| | |
|---|---|
| **DATE:** | Thursday  May 5, 1988 |
| **TIME:** | 8 pm |
| **PLACE:** | Los Gatos Neighborhood Center<br>208 E. Main St.<br>Los Gatos |

### Admission is FREE
Coffee from the Los Gatos Coffee Roasting Company

Presented by

## LOS GATOS PEACE FORUM

P.O. BOX 431 • LOS GATOS 95031

## INSIDE

**CENTER NEWS** January 1991

ALBERT L. SCHULTZ
JEWISH COMMUNITY
CENTER
655 ARASTRADERO ROAD
PALO ALTO, CALIFORNIA
94306

# Tolstoy Lecture

On Sunday, January 13 Michael Levin, a Russian emigré who now resides in Los Altos, will present a lecture on the "Life of Leo Tolstoy." The presentation, which is free, will be held in the Senior Adult Community Room.

Levin has spent much of his life studying and researching the writings of Tolstoy. He will include slides in his presentation.

**LECTURE ON
LEO TOLSTOY
Sunday, January 13 — 7-9pm
No charge**

Michael Levin, a Russian emigré now living in the U.S. presents a slide show lecture and discussion of the life and times of the great Russian writer. Join us for a fascinating evening.

# HIGHLIGHTS OF TOLSTOY'S LIFE

**Born: 8/28/1828** at Yasnaya Polyana, near town of Tula, about 180 miles southwest of Moscow. Had three brothers: Nicolai, Sergei, Dimitry; one sister: Maria.

**March 18, 1830:** Death of Tolstoy's mother (Maria Nicolayevna).

**1833:** The idea of the "Ant Brotherhood" -Green Stick.

**1837:** Death of Father (Nikolai Ilyitch)

**1841:** Family moves to Kazan.

**1844:** Becomes a student of Turkish, Arabic Languages in the Philosophical Faculty of Kazan University.

**1845:** Transfers to Law Faculty. Ceases to believe in prayer or go to church.

**1846:** Becomes dissatisfied with his manner of life.

**1847:** Leaves the University and stays at Yasnaya Polyana.

**1848:** Starts school for Peasant children at Yasnaya Polyana.

**1851: May 2:** Departs for the Caucasus – writing "Childhood". September "The Cossacks" begun.

**1854: September 26.** Tolstoy reaches Sevastopol. War between Russia and Turkey.

**1855:** Tolstoy returns to Petersburg.

**1856: Jan.** Death of brother Dimitry.

**1857: Feb–Aug.** – Journey Aboard – "Lucerne".

**1859: Jan.** "Three Deaths".

**1861: May.** Quarrels with Turgenev about charity. Establishes school at Yasnaya Polyana. Goes to Paris, London – writes: "Holstomyr".

**1862: Oct. 5:** Marries Sofia Andreyevna Berns.

**1863: Jan.** "The Cossacks".

**1864:** "War and Peace" begun.

**1869:** "War and Peace" finished.

**1870:** Studied Greek.

**1873: March:** "Anna Karenina" begun.

**1877:** Final instalments of "Anna Karenina".

**1878: June 15:** renews relations with Turgenev; writing "Confessions".

**1880:** Changing point of view. "Alas" he is writing some sort of religious discussion. He reads and thinks until his head aches, and all to show how incompatible the Church is with the Gospel teachings. Hardly ten people in Russia will be interested in it, but nothing can be done about it. I only wish he would make and finish it and it will pass like an illness." (Letter from Countess).

**1881:** "What Men Live By". Autumn: Family settles in a rented house in Moscow.

**1882:** Writes, "The Census in Moscow". Studies Hebrew with Rabbi Minor.

**1883: Jan.** "He is a leader; one who goes ahead of the crowd, pointing the way men should go. But I am the crowd; I live in its current.. I cannot go faster; I am held by the crowd and by my environment and habits." (Letter from Countess)

"My friend - great writer of the Russian land return to literature - listen to my appeal."

Letter from Turgenev.

**1885:** Becomes vegetarian; gives up hunting; gives up tobacco.

**1889:** "The Kreutzer Sonata"

**1893:** "The Kingdom of God is Within You."

**1897:** "What is Art."

**1899:** "Letter on Hague Conference." Refuse to participate.

"Resurrection."

**1901: March 7 – "**Decree of Excommunication" from the church.

**1909:** The visit of Henry George's son.

**1910:** Thomas Edison visits Moscow to present Tolstoy with a phonograph and record his voice.

**1910: October 28.** Leaves Yasnaya Polyana.

7 November at 0605 hours: Death. Buried at Yasnaya Polyana without religious ceremonies.

"The simplest grave in the world."

Stefan Zweig.

# The Tolstoy Family

Leo (Lev) Nikolayevitch Tolstoy (1828-1910)
Sofia Andryevna (Sonya) (1844-1919)

## Sons:

| | | |
|---|---|---|
| Sergei | – | 7/1863-1947 |
| Ilya | – | 5/1866-1933 |
| Lev | – | 6/1869-1945 |
| Piotr | – | 6/1872-1873 |
| Nicolai | – | 4/1874-1875 |
| Andrei | – | 12/1877-1916 |
| Mikhail | – | 1/1/1880-1944 |
| Aleksei | – | 11/12/1881-1886 |
| Ivan | – | 4/12/1888-1895 |

## Daughters:

| | | |
|---|---|---|
| Tatiana | – | 10/1864-1950 |
| Maria | – | 2/1871-1906 |
| Alexandra | – | 6/30/1884-1979 |

Details of Tolstoy's life can be found in many books.

## A VISIT TO ALEXANDRA TOLSTOY

The date was February 5, 1977. I had been in the United States three months and had been unsuccessfully trying to gain a meeting with Alexandra Tolstoy, the youngest and favorite daughter of the great Russian writer Leo Tolstoy. Finally the Tolstoy Foundation office in New York had given me a number for the Tolstoy Foundation Center in New York's Rockland County. I put in a call and Tatiana Schaufuss, Alexandra Tolstoy's longtime friend, picked up the phone. I introduced myself, explaining that I was a Moscow native who for the seven years had been a tour guide at Yasnaya Polyana, Tolstoy's birthplace and family estate, and that I would like to meet and talk with Miss Tolstoy.

Miss Schaufuss wanted to know how I got this private phone number, and also told me that I had to have an appointment to see Miss Tolstoy. At my explanation, she invited me to visit Miss Tolstoy on February 12 and to have dinner with her first.

The date finally came. I went to the Fort Washington station at the end of the subway and purchased a ticket on bus 9A leaving at 1:10 p.m. This was my first trip out of New York City. Up until then I had thought the United States was wall-to-wall skyscrapers, but now I saw cottages and plenty of greenery and lakes. In 50 minutes I was at the farm of Alexandra Tolstoy. At the reception office of the Center I was met by Miss Schaufuss and Cyril Galitzine of the Tolstoy Foundation and ushered into dinner: chicken bouillon with noodles, chicken with mashed potatoes, fruit compote, and black coffee.

They asked me where I hailed from, about my arrival in the U.S., and what I was doing now. My mention of Moscow called up many reminiscences. They also wanted to know if Lubyanka Prison was still in Moscow, and if the Spassaky Gate Tower still stood. Tatiana Schaufuss observed that she had spent time in Lubyanka.

On another occasion, she related, she had asked Feliks Dzerjinsky, head of the secret police, for permission to set up a commission under the aegis of the Red Cross to investigate unjust sentences in the Soviet Union. He did not grant permission. He told her that he signed many death sentences every day. Then he pulled out a photograph of his son, a small boy dressed in a sailor suit such as children of the aristocracy had once worn. As he showed it to her, he added, "And if it became necessary, I would give the order to shoot him."

While we were on the subject of Soviet leaders, she mentioned that Yakov Sverdlov, one of the leaders of the 1917 revolution and a Jew, had been buried at his death in 1919 according to Jewish traditions despite his official atheism.

She asked me what I knew about Jewish customs. I replied that though I was a Jew I had lived all my life among Russians, so I didn't know much about the customs. "Jews know Russia better than the Russians themselves," she commented. Then she recounted how one day a Jew came to her and told her that he had converted to Christianity and showed her the cross around his neck. She was both surprised and angered, for as she observed, "I didn't ask him to change his religion."

After about 25 minutes of conversation Miss Schaufuss invited me to visit the White House, where she lived with Miss Tolstoy. It was a small one-story wooden cottage. Alexandra Tolstoy was seated at the dining table in the kitchen. She wore glasses and very much resembled her father. I came up to her and kissed her hand and gave her the presents I had brought: a little samovar on a tray, a copy of the samovar which stood in the dining room in Yasnaya Polyana, and postcards with views of Tula, a town near the estate.

Before we got into conversation Tatiana Schaufuss offered to show me the house. Alexandra Tolstoy's main living space was a small, cozy living room and a bedroom. Most of the objects in them were intimately connected with the life of her famous father. The photos on the wall were reminders of her days in Yasnaya Polyana. There was a Russian motto in large letters: *"The soul is at peace and rest when all the family shares the same nest."* Through a big window in the living room she could see the garden and watch the birds and squirrels at their feeders.

A second living room-bedroom suite belonging to Tatiana Schaufuss was more modern. There were many books on subjects related to art and religion, including one on Jewish art and biographies of Golda Meir and Moshe Dayan. Icons stood in the corners.

After my tour of the house I was seated at the dining-room table with Alexandra Tolstoy. Tatiana Schaufuss introduced me and explained who I was and where I had come from. I described my last visit to Yasnaya Polyana. Alexandra Tolstoy asked me about the school, which she herself had set up. The buildings, she said, were copies of those in Kaluga, a famous historical town about a hundred miles from Moscow. She had copied the plans for reconstructing them at Yasnaya Polyana. She had also personally planted many of the trees there.

"Would you like to return to your birthplace?" I asked.

"Very much," she replied. "I dream of gathering mushrooms there as I did with my father in my childhood. But I never will, for two reasons. First, many people in the Soviet Union would like to see me dead; and, second, if I were to go, the Russian government would think that I had compromised and recognized them. Unfortunately, many cruel things still go on there.

"Do you know what the 'wardrobe' is?" she asked.

I nodded and spread my arms wide to indicate size.

"Do you think it possible for a person to fit inside one?" Only then did I realize that she was referring not to a piece of furniture but to a small box where prisoners were kept for hours as a form of punishment.

Michael Levin at Tolstoy Foundation Center, Lake Road,
Valley Cottage, New York, February 5, 1977.
(He had arrived in New York City from Moscow, Russia, on
November 17, 1976.)

"Why does Brezhnev (Leonid Brezhnev, then General Secretary of the Communist Party of Russia) lead the life he does? He drinks and indulges in drunken orgies. Is something telling him that it's time for a change?" I found it difficult to answer such questions. I only knew that in Brezhnev's time many dissidents had been arrested.

"President Carter is such a nice man," Alexandra Tolstoy went on. "He believes everything," she said referring to Carter's efforts for rapprochement with Russia.

Our talk turned to emigres. "One day an emigre architect visited me. He asked me to help him find work. I asked what was the English word for the Russian word meaning 'beam'. He could not answer. How could he work as a architect in the United States? He will need to start all over from the beginning."

Later Tatiana Schaufuss would add her own story. "When Solzhenitsyn (the writer Alexander Solzhenitsyn) came here he spent all of his time making calls from our phone and taking care of his own business," she said.

"Are you very familiar with the house of the Volkonskys?" This was the home of the family of Tolstoy's maternal grandmother (and it had been Yasnaya Polyana's estate.) "I planted many trees there and also drew up plans for each field."

Now we were on writing. "My father had tremendous understanding of human nature and every person in his books shared in that part of his character. He did not really like *War and Peace*. He felt it was too complicated for most people. The work he liked best was the short tale "What Men Live By". In it my father expressed his philosophy of life, which was very simple: Love your neighbor and treat him as you would wish to be treated."

"I frequently receive letters from schoolgirls in Yasnaya Polyana. Such nice girls! What can I send them? What do you think? Would it put them in danger to receive a present from the United States?"

I assured her that it would be very good if she could send the girls a photo of herself and one of her father, and she accepted my suggestion.

Alexandra Tolstoy offered to help me find a job, but I answered that I had not come there for that but to see her. "Why do you refuse our offer?" Tatiana Schaufuss put in. "We will help you now and you will help someone else later. Once I got sick and people started sending me money. One sent five dollars. Others sent ten or fifteen. At the beginning this upset me, but after a time I realized that there was nothing demeaning about it. We give help in the same spirit."

I had brought with me a portrait of Leo Tolstoy which I had purchased in a famous Moscow book store on Kalinin Prospect. I expressed the hope that Alexandra Tolstoy would autograph it for me. She took the portrait and, looking at it for two or three minutes, seemed lost in thought. "What can I write?

Ah, I will find a motto from my father's book *Day by Day* (in which he gave guidelines for everyday life. M. L.)."

I did not want to leave, but Tatiana Schaufuss had warned me not to talk too long and tire Miss Tolstoy. As I rose I asked whether they ever needed help with heavy work. Miss Tolstoy answered that soon the snow would melt and they would start to plant tomatoes. Several years ago she had planted them herself but now, she said, if you can come to help, I will sit on the sidelines and give instructions. I said I would come when they wanted me and she gave me her private phone number. Unfortunately, I never had the chance to help her. The next time I went to her home was for her funeral a year and a half later.

With an expression of graditude for her warm reception, I took one last look at the portrait which I was leaving for her to sign, and left. A few weeks later I received the portrait back with the words:

*My father once said: "Believing gives soulful peace; sense of divine soul gives power" These words of his have always helped me in life. And I am happy that you helped people - tourists - when they came to bow their heads at his grave.*

*Thank You!*
*Alexandra Tolstoy (92 years).*
*18 February. 1977.*

The next photos are from the funeral of Alexandra Tolstoy taken on October 1, 1979, in Valley Cottage, New York, taken by Michael Levin.

Michael Levin – third from left

Tatiana Schaufuss, lifelong friend of Alexandra Tolstoy

Tatiana Schaufuss

Alexandra Tolstoy in her coffin

Coffin of Alexandra is closed

The gravesite is closed
(Who is this girl?)

The cross on the grave of Alexandra Tolstoy.
It is written in Russian:
"Alexandra Lvovna Tolstaia 1.VII. 1884 – 26. IX. 1979"

## CONCLUSION

After spending so much time reading and studying Tolstoy, we have come to various conclusions which we feel we must mention here.

Tolstoy felt that dividing up the world into countries was basically against all that Christ has ever taught. That doing so with people caused nothing but death and destruction. Putting up fences was evil.

And so, when Tolstoy began to be seen as inappropriate, he was already trying to give all of his land to his serfs, against the wishes of his wife, friends and relatives.

This was a man who did not gravitate towards possessions. This was a man who loved to ride his bicycle, who had a walking stick which he used on his many walks, who enjoyed his ice skates and truly felt that music and music alone was a savior for his sanity and the world's. The trappings of his wealthy class, seen all about him, seemed to give little meaning to his daily being and were as if a part of his wife's world and not his own.

Tolstoy feared the wars of the world so very keenly after his own experiences spoken of in War and Peace, but after the new century arrived, all these powerful things that men could do to one another loomed over him and he spoke exhaustively about "peace meetings".

His viewpoint on these meetings always came to one conclusion: that all the "little" talks that went on and ended up with death one way or another, were "babblings" and nothing more. Of course, his seeing this almost 100 years ago makes him more right than right for today's worldly problems.

In speaking of peaceful co-existence and Christian behavior, of "turn the other cheek", we have to remember that there would have been no Gandhi as we know him today, if it were not for Tolstoy. And, of course, Martin Luther King followed Gandhi dramatically and affected an entire nation here in the United States.

At the core of all this compassion lies Tolstoy's unusual view of charity. He almost lost his life in a duel over his disagreement with Turgenev's, the famous Russian writer, beliefs on this subject.

Christ believed in turning the other cheek. And Tolstoy wrote about loving your enemy which was certainly difficult. He believed that this was the proof of one's love. Regarding charity, he saw that just giving money to an unknown face does not really prove much about Christian soul of givers.

For giving charity in money, not seeing or knowing the person you are trying to help, is, in a way, an absenteeism style of compassion. As long as you don't get dirty or experience a hardship, giving away a little extra money which is not in any way painful for the contributor, seems to be fine. Tolstoy felt this was not fine.

He felt that charity is not charity but a charade. It proves nothing. He always felt that living as a rich man and giving alms (charity) in tiny pieces to the poor around you was despicable. He felt that the poor should be sitting right next to you and you should be working right with them in the fields. And that truly everyone should be eating the same and sleeping in the same style.

Can you imagine how unpopular this was for the Tsar to hear from a man whose family had for 20 or so generations been famous and powerful? And, of course, so much of this was a forerunner to communism.

But, it is not communism we speak of here. We are saying, and it pertains ever so dramatically to today, that when others are so vastly wealthy, the poor should not be so poor or so hungry. And that is what Christianity is all about.

Can you imagine Tolstoy's feelings about "hands across America" and singing a song for millions of starving people in the U. S. and elsewhere? Where does the charities' money go? And how do we know that any of it really gets to the people? As is seen in the past, the government doesn't allow it to be spent properly and much of it sits in the bank collecting interest. Who gets that interest? Tolstoy felt that in being charitable and Christian, one had to get personally involved. All the people come home with souvenirs of their charitable moment. Did anyone of them share a meal with a homeless person? Did anyone bring a homeless person home? Would Christ have found them too dirty to have around?

That brings us to Christianity. You see, Tolstoy had rewritten the gospels and gotten himself excommunicated from the Church. He felt they had too many icons and procedures, and he still saw serfs hungry with substandard homes.

It is hard to truly count the people who worshiped him from afar or those who visited to sit at his feet and be with the "great thinker". Yet his government and religious persons were against him. His wife was against him.

His wife did not want to share him with anyone. And she wanted to have power to earn money from all of his writings. Sophy Behrs was not a Tolstoy, but she had married into a well to do family and certainly, she would never give up this wealth.

What could it have been like for a man to be married to a beautiful woman, a woman who copied all of his greatest works, yet a woman who did not concur with his deepest wishes and dreams? She helped him so much that the world came to know him for what he was. Yet, when it was most important for her to understand, he left her behind.

So, we have a man so taken with the real meaning of Christ, and finding himself, in his deepest soul, almost not worthy enough. For Tolstoy had at one time sought after women and war and wealth and his great discovery, the truth of Christ and one's relation to him, upset him greatly. He no longer wanted to be the Tolstoy he had once started to be.

This passion to carve up his religion as he knew it and reorganize it to renew his peace, twisted and tormented his soul. And out of all this torment, we find the man who was truly great. Beyond the author and thinker, we find an educator and a being so human and so kind; he almost didn't belong in his country or his time.

But where do we put Tolstoy? Is there a category for him? Are there people to put with him?

Tolstoy should be studied and learned from. His values can encourage us and give us a future full of hope.

Works of Tolstoy's recommended to readers are:

*Childhood*
*Youth*
*The Snowstorm*
*Boyhood*
*The Cossacks*
*Sevastopol in May*
*Sevastopol in August*
*Strider*
*A Morning of a Landlord*
*Resurrection*

*What Men Live By*

*The Kingdom of God is Within You*

*Lucerne*

*Three Deaths*

*Polikushka*

*War and Peace*

*Anna Karenina*

*The Power of Darkness*

*The Fruits of Enlightenment*

*The Kreutzer Sonata*

*Hadji Murat*

*Confession*

*On Art*

*What Must We Do?*

*Answer to Synod on Excommunication from Church*

Some of these books were banned in many countries. *The Kreutzer Sonata* was banned in the United States.

# Additional Photos

November 16, 1993.
The limousine of President of Russia Boris N. Yeltzin at the entrance to Yasnaya Polyana where Leo Tolstoy was born, lived a long life, and is buried.

November 16, 1993.
President of Russia Boris N. Yeltzin visits Leo Tolstoy's grave at Yasanaya Polyana.

132

November 16, 1993.
President of Russia Boris N. Yeltsin places flowers on the grave of Leo Tolstoy.

Parents of Michael Levin.
Moscow, February 1929. Asia Levin (1907-1990), Leizer Tetievskiy (1898-1982)

Standing top left, is the father of Michael Levin with his friends.
Moscow, Russia, 1923

Leizer Tetievskiy in Moscow, 1929.

Asia Levin in Moscow, 1929.

Summer 1947.
Misha (Michael) Levin, 9 years old. Settlement Yelenskoye, Moscow District, Russia.

Michael Levin in 1964, Moscow, Russia.

## ⋆WHAT MEN LIVE BY (1881)

*We know that we have passed out of death unto life, because we love the brethren. He that loveth not abideth in death. 1 Epistle John, iii. 14.*

*Whoso hath the world's good, and beholdeth his brother in need, and shutteth up his compassion from him, how doth the love of God abide in him? My little children, let us not love in word, neither with the tongue, but in deed and truth. - iii. 17-18.*

*Love is of God, and every one that loveth is begotten of God, and knoweth God. He that loveth not, knoweth not God, for God is love. - iv. 7-8.*

*No man hath beheld God at any time, if we love one another, God abideth in us. - iv. 12.*

*God is love, and he that abideth in love abideth in God, and God abideth in him. - iv. 16.*

*If a man say, I love God, and hateth his brother, he is a liar, for he that loveth not his brother whom he hath seen, how can he love God whom he hath not seen? - iv. 20.*

⋆ Per my conversation with Alexandra Tolstoy, this story was the writing that pleased Tolstoy more than <u>War and Peace</u>. The story gives something for the soul and the mind and it reflects what Tolstoy more than <u>War and Peace</u> .The story givessomething for the soul and the mind and it reflects what Tolstoy believe in.

A shoemaker, with his wife and children, lived in a farmer's house. He had neither house nor land of his own, and he supported himself and his family by his cobbling. Bread was dear, and work cheap; and what he made by work went into the food. The shoemaker and his wife had one sheepskin coat between them, and that was falling into rags, and this was the second year the shoemaker had been wanting to buy sheepskins for a new sheepskin coat

By autumn the shoemaker had gathered together a little money; three paper rubles were hidden in his wife's box, and besides that there were five rubles and twenty-five kopecks due from the farmers in the village.

So one cold morning the shoemaker got himself ready to go to the village for his sheepskin. He put on, over his shirt, the wadded jacket which his wife had made for herself not long before, and over that his belted cloth coat; he put his three-ruble note in his pocket, cut himself a stick, and departed after breakfast. He though to himself; "I shall get my five rubles from the farmers, I'll add these three to them, and I'll buy sheepskins for a sheepkin coat."

So the shoemaker went into the village and stopped by at one of the farmers; he was not at home. His wife promised to send her husband to him with the money in a week. He went on to another. This farmer took God to witness that he had noo money. He gave him only twenty kopecks for mending his boots. The shoemaker though of getting the sheepskins on credit, but fur-dealer would not let him have any on credit. "Bring the money," said he, "and then take what you like. We know how debts mount up." So the shoemaker did no business that day. He only got twenty kopecks for mending the boots, and he took away another pair of old boots for resoling.

The shoemaker was greatly depressed. He drank away the whole of the twenty kopecks in vodka, and set off home without his sheepskins. He had hand. And as he went along, he talked to himself.

"I'm warm without a sheepskin coat," said he, "I've drunk a thimbleful and it skips about through all my veins. So a sheepskin is not necessary after all. Here I go along and forget all my troubles. That's the sort of chap I am. What do I care? I can get along without sheepskins. I didn't need them. There's one thing, though – that wife of mine will fret about it. She'll say: 'Tis a shame you work for him and he leads you by the nose.' Wait a bit, that's all! If you don't bring me my money, you farmer, I'll take the very cap from your head, by God I will! What sort of pay is this? He palms off a couple of kopecks on me! What's a man to do with a couple of kopecks? Drink it up, and be done with it. 'I'm hard up,' says he. You're hard up, are you, and don't you suppose that I am hard up too? You have a house and cattle and everything else, and all I have is on my back! You make your own flour, I have to buy mine. Get it from wherever I can; three rubles I must have to spend on flour every week. I go home and all the bread is gone. Again I have to lay out a ruble and a half. Why can't you give me my money, and no nonsense!"

Thus the shoemaker went on till he came to the shrine at the corner. He looked, and close up by the shrine something was glistening white. It was just then beginning to be twilight. The shoemaker looked at it more narrowly, but he could not make out what it was.

"There's no such stone as that there!" thought he. "A cow, perhaps? But it's not like a cow either. It has got a head like a man. It's something white or other. But what would a man be doing here?"

He drew nearer. It was now quite visible. What marvel was this? It was indeed a man sitting there quite naked. Who shall say whether he was alive or dead? He was leaning against the shrine, and didn't move. The shoemaker felt queer. He said to himself: "They have killed some man, rifled his pockets, and pitched him out here. You go on, and don't mix yourself up with it!"

So the shoemaker went on. He went in back of the shrine so the man was longer to be seen. He passed by the shrine and looked round; there was the man leaning forward, and moving a little as if he were looking towards the shoemaker. The shoemaker became still more afraid, and he thought to himself: "Shall I go up to him or shall I pass by? Go to him, indeed! Some evil may come of it! Who knows who and what he is? No good errand has brought him here, I can tell you that! Maybe he'll leap at me, and throttle me, and do harm to me. And even if he doesn't, whatever can I do with a naked man? I can't give him the very last rags off my own back, I suppose? God help me while I pass by him, that's all!"

And the shoemaker quickened his pace. He was already passing the shrine when his conscience began to nip him. And the shoemaker stood still in the middle of the road.

"What ails the man?" said he to himself. "What are you doing, Simon? Here's a man dying in misery and you take fright and pass him by? Have you grown rich, maybe? Do you fear they'll steal your treasures? Come, come, Simon, this won't do!"

*          *          *

Simon went up to the man, looked carefully at him and saw that he was young and strong, with no bruises on his body; but it was plain that the man was half frozen and full of fear -- there he sat, leaning against the wall and did not even look at Simon, as if he were too weak to raise his eyes. Simon went close up to him, and, suddenly, as if the man had only just awoke, he turned his head, opened his eyes, and looked at Simon. This look quite endeared the man to Simon. He threw the boots he was carrying to the ground, took off his belt, placed it on the boots, and drew off his coat.

"Can you talk a bit?" said he. "Never mind! Come, put this on!"

Simon took the man by the elbow and helped to lift him up. The man got up, and Simon saw that his body was slender and clean, that his hands and feet had no bruises upon them, and his face was pleasant to look upon. Simon threw his coat over the man's shoulders, but the man could not manage the sleeves. So Simon put his hands right for him, stroked down and buttoned up the coat, and belted it with the belt.

Simon also took his tattered cap from his head to put it on the bare head of the man, but his own head went quite cold, and he thought to himself: "I am bald all over my head, but he has long hair," and he put on his hat again. "Twould be better if I gave him the boots to wear," said he.

So he made him sit down, and put the old boots onto the man's feet.

Thus the shoemaker dressed him, and said: "There you are, brother! Come now, try and move about a bit and warm yourself. You will feel all right in a minute. Don't you think you can walk by yourself?"

The man stood up, looked kindly at Simon, but could not speak a word.

"Why don't you speak? We can't pass all of the winter What Men Live By here. We must be getting home. Look here now! Here's my wooden stick! Lean on it if you feel weak. Off we go!"

So the man set off. He walked easily, and never lagged behind.

As they went along the road, Simon said, "Where are you from?"

"I am not of this place."

"So I see, for I know everyone who lives here. But how then did you come to be at the shrine?"

"I may not tell you."

"I suppose the people here ill-treated you?"

"Nobody has ill-treated me, but God has punished me."

"Yes, indeed -- God is over all, and everywhere His hand is upon us. But where would you like to go?"

"It's all one to me."

Simon was amazed. The man was gentle of speech, and not like a rogue, and yet he would give no account of himself; and Simon thought:

"One little knows what sort of things go on in this world."

And he said to the man: "Look now, come to my house and warm yourself up a bit."

So Simon went on, and the stranger never left him, but kept along side of him. The wind arose and found its way beneath Simon's shirt; the drink he had taken was now pretty well out of him, and he began to feel freezing cold. On he went, snuffling loudly and wrapping his wife's jacket more closely around him, and he thought to himself: "That's what your sheepskin has brought you to. You went out for a sheepskin, and you come back without a coat, and bring a naked man home with you besides. Your old Matrena will not bless you for it!"

And the moment he fell to thinking of his wife Matrena, he grew uncomfortable. But when he looked at the stranger he remembered how the man looked at him at the shrine, and his heart leaped up within him.

\*             \*             \*

Simon's wife was ready early. She chopped the firewood, brought in the water, fed the children, took a bit herself, and began to think: "When shall I make the bread, now or tomorrow?" A big piece still remained.

"If Simon has had something to eat down in town," she thought, "and doesn't eat much for supper, there will be enough bread to go on with till tomorrow."

Matrena kept turning the piece of bread round and round, and she thought: "I won't make the bread now. There's only enough flour left for one loaf. We can manage to get along till Friday."

Matrena put away the bread, and sat down at the table to sew a patch onto her husband's shirt. She sewed and sewed. And all the time she thought of her husband, and how he had gone to buy sheepskins for a coat.

"I hope the sheepskin-seller won't cheat him, for my old man really is very simple. He cheats nobody himself, but a little child might lead him by the nose. Eight rubles. That is no small amount of money; we should get a pretty good sheepskin coat for it. I went through last winter as best I could without a sheepskin coat. I could go nowhere, not even to the brook. And look now! He has left the house, and has put on every stitch we have. I have nothing to put on at all. He's a long time coming. 'Tis time he was here now. I hope my little one has not gone astray somewhere."

While Matrena was still thinking over these thoughts, there was a scraping on the outer staircase; somebody was coming in. Matrena stuck her needle into her work, and went out into the passage. She looked. Two were there, –Simon, and with him some sort of a man without a cap, and in felt boots.

All at once Matrena noticed the breath of her husband. "Yes, that's it," she thought, "he's been drinking." And when she perceived that he was without his long coat, in the jacket only, and carried nothing in his hand, and was silent, but pulled a wry face, Matrena's heart was hot within her. "He has drunk away the money," she thought; "he has been wandering about with some vagabond or other, and has gone so far as to bring him home with him. Matrena let them go into the room, and came in herself also. She perceived that the man was a stranger – young, haggard; the coat he had on was theirs; he had none. He stood on the spot where he had first come in, neither moving nor raising his eyes. And Matrena thought: "He is not a good man, for he is afraid."

Matrena wrinkled her brows, went up to the oven, and waited to see what they would do next.

Simon took off his hat and sat down on the bench as if all were well.

"Well, Matrena!" said he, "give us some supper, come!"

Matrena grumbled to herself, but kept standing by the oven as if she never meant to move from it. First she looked at the one, and then she looked at the other, but she only shook her head.

Simon saw that his wife was very angry; but what was to be done? He pretended to notice nothing and took the stranger by the arm.

"Sit down, brother!" said he, "and we'll have some supper."

The stranger sat down on the bench.

"Come now, have you cooked anything?"

Matrena grew angry.

"Cooked I have, but not for you. I see you have drunk your sense away. You went for a sheepskin coat and have come back without your own, and have brought back some naked beggar with you into the bargain. I have no supper to give a pair of drunkards."

"Let be Matrena! Your tongue wags and wags. But first you should ask what manner of man it is."

"It is you who should say what you have done with our money."

Simon fumbled in his jacket, drew out the paper money, and unfolded it.

"The money -- there it is; but Trifonov has given me nothing, he said he would give it to me soon."

Matrena grew still angrier. He had not bought the sheepskins, and he had given his only coat to some naked rascal, and even brought him home with him.

She took the paper money from the table, stowed it away about her person, and said:

"You'll get no supper from me. You can't afford to feed all the naked drunkards who run against you."

"Ah! Matrena, put a gag on your tongue. Listen first of all to what people say to you."

"What! Listen to reason from a drunken fool? How right I was when I refused to be your wife at first, you sot, you! My mother gave me lots of linen -- you drank it away. You went to buy sheepskins -- you drank that money away too."

Simon wanted to explain to his wife that he had only drunk twenty kopecks' worth; he wanted to say how he had fallen in with the man; but Matrena didn't give him the chance of speaking a word or finding an answer -- she spoke two words to his one. She even brought up against him again what had happened ten years before.

Matrena talked and talked, and then she made a rush at Simon and caught him by the sleeve.

"Give me back my jacket! That is all I have left, and you've taken it from me and put it on your own back. Give it to me, you mangy dog! May you die of a stroke!"

Simon drew off the jacket and pulled one of the sleeves the wrong side out. Then his wife tugged at it, and almost tore it asunder at the seams. Matrena snatched up the jacket, threw it over her head, and made for the door. She would have gone out, but stopped short, for her heart was sore within her. She was bubbling over with evil unspoken, and she wanted to know besides who this strange man was.

*          *          *

Matrena stood still, and said, "If he were a good man he would not be naked like that. Why, he hasn't even got a shirt to his back. And if you had been about any honest business, you would have said where you picked up such a fine fellow!"

"I'll tell you then. I was going along. I passed by the shrine, and there sat this man, all naked and frozen. It is not summer-time, now, that a man should go about naked. Would he not have perished if God had not brought me to him? What was to be done now? Was it such a small matter to leave him?

I took him, clothed him, and brought him home. Don't be so angry then. It is a sin, Matrena. We shall die one day."

Matrena would have liked to scold some more, but she looked at the stranger and was silent. The stranger was sitting down, but he didn't move. He was sitting on the edge of the bench. His arms were clasped together on his knees, his head had sunk down upon his breast; he did not open his eyes, and his face was all in folds and wrinkles, as if something was suffocating him. Then Simon spoke:

"Matrena! Is there nothing of God within you?"

Matrena heard this sentence, looked again at the stranger, and suddenly her heart was moved. She left the door, went to the corner where the oven was, and got some supper. She put a cup on the table, poured out some hot soup, and brought forth their last piece of bread. Then she put down a knife and two spoons.

"Will you taste of our bread?" said she.

Simon nudged the stranger.

"Sit here, good youth!" he said.

Simon cut the bread, crumbled it into the soup, and fell to supper. But Matrena sat at the corner of the table, rested her head on her elbows, and looked at the stranger.

And Matrena felt sorry for the stranger, and began to like him. And suddenly the stranger grew more cheerful. He ceased to wrinkle his face, he raised his eyes toward Matrena, and smiled.

They finished supper; the good wife cleared away, and began to question the stranger:

"Whence do you come?"

"I am not of this place."

"Then how came you along this road?"

"I cannot say."

"Has any man robbed you?"

"God has punished me."

"And you were lying naked like that?"

"I was lying naked like that, and freezing. Simon saw and had compassion upon me; he took off his long coat, clothed me with it, and bade me come hither. And here you have had pity upon me, and given me to eat and drink. The Lord bless you."

Matrena rose up, took from the window Simon's old shirt, the same shirt she had mended, and gave it to the stranger. She also hunted up some old trousers of Simon's and these she gave him likewise.

"There you are, take them! I see you have no shirt. Put them on, and lie down in the loft. Matrena put out the lamp, took the coat and joined her husband at the oven.

Matrena lay down and covered herself with the skirts of the coat, but could not sleep; she could not get the stranger out of her thoughts at all.

When she reflected that he had eaten up their last bit of bread, and there was no bread for the morrow, and that she had given away the shirt and the trousers, she was very vexed; then she recollected how he had smiled, and her heart went forth to him.

For a long time Matrena could not sleep, but lay listening. Simon also could not sleep, and drew the coat towards his side of the oven.

"Simon!"

"Eh?"

"We have eaten our last bit of bread. I have made no more. I don't know how it will be tomorrow. I'll have to borrow a little from our neighbor, Malania."

"We shall live and be satisfied."

The woman lay back and was silent.

"The man is a good man, that's clear, only why is he so quiet about himself?"

"Perhaps he has to be?"

"Why?"

"Ah!"

"We give him what we have, but why does nobody give to us?"

Simon knew not what to answer her. "Just let us stop talking!" he said. Then he turned himself round and went to sleep.

\*           \*           \*

In the morning Simon awoke. The children were asleep; his wife had gone to the neighbors to borrow flour. Only the stranger of the evening before, in the old trousers and the shirt, was sitting on the bench and looking upwards. His face was even brighter than the evening before, and Simon said:

"Look now, good fellow, the belly begs for bread and the naked body for clothing. You must work for food and clothes. What trade do you know?"

"I know nothing."

Simon was amazed, and he said:

"Where there's a will to do it, a man can learn anything."

"All men work, and I will work too."

"What is your name?"

"Michael."

"Well, Michael, you won't tell us anything about yourself, and that's your business, but you must eat. If you will work as I tell you, then I'll feed you."

"The Lord preserve you. I will learn. Show me what to do."

Simon took a piece of waxed thread, put it around his fingers, and began to twist the ends of it.

Michael looked on, took it in his fingers and began to twist the ends of it in the same way. Then

Simon showed him how to welt the leather, and Michael understood it at once. Then his host showed him how to sew pieces of leather together, and how to clip them straight, and this also Michael understood at once.

Whatever work Simon showed him, he understood it immediately, and after three days he worked as if he had been at it all his life. He worked without blundering, and ate little. He worked without a break, kept silent and always looked upwards. He never went out in the road, never spoke a word too much, and neither laughed nor joked.

They had seen him smile only once, and that was on the first evening when Matrena had given him some supper.

\*                    \*                    \*

Day by day week by week, the year went round. Michael lived as before at Simon's and worked. And the fame of Simon's workman went forth, and they said that nobody could sew boots together so cleanly and so strongly as Simon's workman Michael. They began to come to Simon for boots from the whole countryside, and Simon began to prosper in his trade.

One day, in the winter-time, Simon and Michael were sitting working together, when a three-horse sleigh, with all its bells ringing, dashed up to the house. They looked out of the window; the sleigh stopped at their door; a young servant leaped down from the seat, and opened the door of the sleigh. Out of the sleigh stepped a gentleman wrapped up in a fur coat. He got out of the sleigh and went to Simon's house, and mounted the staircase. Matrena darted out and threw the door wide open.

The gentleman stooped his head down to pass under the doorway, and entered. When he stood upright his head very nearly touched the ceiling, and his body took up a whole corner of the room.

Simon stood up and bowed deeply. He was much surprised to see the gentleman there. He had never seen such a fine gentleman. Now Simon was quite lean, and Michael was thin, and Matrena was like a dried bone; but this person was like a man from another world; his big fat face was red, his neck was like a bull's; his whole frame looked as though made out of cast iron.

The gentleman breathed heavily; took off his furs; sat down on the bench, and said: "Who's the master here?"

Simon stepped forward and said: "I am, your honor."

The gentleman shouted to his lad: "Fedka, bring the leather."

The servant came running in with a bundle. The gentleman took the bundle and placed it on the table. "Open it!" said he. The lad opened it.

The gentleman tapped the leather with the tips of his fingers, and said to Simon: "Look here, shoemaker! Do you see this leather?"

"I see it, your excellency!" said Simon.

"Can you tell what sort of leather this is?"

Simon felt the leather a bit and said, "Good stuff!"

"Good stuff! I should rather think so! Why you fool, you've never seen such leather in your life before. German goods; it cost me twenty rubles."

Simon was a little taken aback at this, so he said: "How should we ever see such leather?"

"Of course not. Exactly. Now, can you make me a pair of boots out of this leather?"

"I can, your honor!"

The gentleman raised his voice at him. "You can, can you? Understand clearly what you are going to stitch, and what sort of leather you are working on. You must stitch me a pair of boots which will last me the whole year round, and will neither lose their shape nor come unsewn. If you can do this, take the leather and cut it up; if you can't, don't take the leather, and don't cut it up. I tell you beforehand, if the boots lose their shape or open at the seams before the year is out, I'll clap you in jail; but if they don't lose shape or come unsewn within a year, I'll give you ten rubles for your work."

Simon was a bit afraid and didn't know what to say. He glanced at Michael, nudged him with his elbow, and whispered to him: "What think you, brother?"

Michael nodded his head, as if to say: "Take the work by all means."

Simon followed Michael's advice. He undertook to make boots that would neither lose shape nor come apart. The gentleman called to his lad, ordered him to take his boot off his left leg; then he held out his foot and said: "Take my measure!"

Simon sewed together a piece of paper about seventeen inches long, had a good look at the gentlman's foot, went down on his knees, wiped his hands neatly on his apron so as not to soil the elegant sock, and began to take measures. He took the measure of the sole, he took the measure of the instep, he began to measure the calf, but the piece of measuring paper would not do. The leg was very big in the calf, just like a thick beam.

"Take care you don't pinch me in the shins!" said the gentleman.

Simon took yet another piece of paper to measure with. The gentleman sat down, twiddled his toes about in his stockings; looked round at the people in the hut and perceived Michael.

"Who's that you've got there?"

"That's my apprentice. It is he who will stitch the boots."

"Look now!" said the gentleman to Michael, "be careful how you stitch! The boots must last through the whole year." Simon also looked at Michael. He saw that he was not looking at the gentleman, but was staring at the corner behind the gentleman as if he saw someone there. Michael kept on looking and looking, and all at once he smiled, and his face grew quite bright.

"What are you showing your teeth for, you fool? You had much better see that the things are ready in time!" said the gentleman.

And Michael said: "They'll be quite ready when they're wanted."

"Very well."

The gentleman put on his boot and fur coat, sniffed a bit and went towards the door. But he forgot to stoop, so he hit his head against the lintel. The gentleman cursed, rubbed his forehead, went down the steps, sat himself down in his sleigh, and drove off.

So the gentleman went away.

Then Simon said: "He is hard as a rock. He nearly knocked the beam out with his head and it hardly hurt him a bit."

But Matrena said: "How can he help getting hard and tough with the life he leads? Even death itself has no hold over a rock like that."

*    *    *

And Simon said to Michael: "We have the work, but whether it will do us a mischief after all who can say? The wares are dear, and the gentleman is stern. What if we blunder over it? Look now! Your eyes are sharper than mine, and your hands are defter at measuring. Cut out the leather now, and I'll work on the lining."

Michael obeyed at once. He took the gentleman's leather, spread it out on the table, folded it in two, took his knife, and began to cut it.

Matrena came forward and saw Michael cutting out, and she was amazed at the way in which Michael did it. Matrena was used to the sight of shoemaker's work, and she looked and saw that Michael did not cut out as shoemakers usually do for boots, but rather cut in a circle. Matrena would have liked to speak, but she thought: "Maybe I don't understand how gentleman's boots ought to be cut out. No doubt Michael knows better than I. I won't interfere." Michael had now cut out the leather, and he took up the ends and began to sew; not as shoemakers do with boots, so as to have two ends, but with only one end, like those who make soft slippers for the dead.

Matrena was amazed at this also, but even now she didn't interfere. Michael went on sewing. It began to get dark. Simon got up for supper, and looked around. Out of the gentleman's leather Michael had made, not boots, but slippers.

Simon groaned: "How is it," thought he, "that Michael, who has been working with us for a whole year without making a mistake, has now done us a mischief. The gentleman bespoke heavy soled boots, and he has stitched without soles. He has spoiled the leather. What shall I say to the gentleman? I can never replace leather like this."

And he said to Michael: "What is this you have

done, my friend? You have ruined me. The gentleman bespoke boots, and what have you stitched together here?"

Scarcely had Simon begun to take Michael to task about the boots when there was a fumbling at the door-latch, and someone knocked. They looked out of the window; someone had come on horseback and had just tied up his horse. They opened the door, and in came the servant lad who been with the gentleman.

"Good health to you!"

"Good health! What's amiss?"

"My mistress has sent me about the boots."
"About the boots?"

"Yes, about the boots. Master needs no more boots. He'll never stamp again! He's dead!"

"It's not possible!"

"He didn't even get home alive. He died in the sleigh. When the sleigh got to the house and we went to help him out, there he was like a lump, all of a heap and frozen stiff, lying there dead. It was as much as we could do to tear him from the sleigh. My mistress has sent me saying: 'Tell the shoemaker what has happened. Say, since boots are no longer needed for master, would he make a pair of soft slippers for the body out of the leather.' I am to wait til they are stitched, and then I am to take them back with me. That is why I have come."

Michael took the clippings of the leather from the table and rolled them up into a ball. He took the two slippers, which were quite ready, slapped them one against the other, wiped them with his apron, and gave them to the lad. The lad took away the slippers. "Good-by, master! Good day to you."

     *         *         *

Another year passed by -- two years passed by. It was now the sixth year of MIchael's abiding with Simon. He lived just in the same way as before. He went nowhere, and spoke to no stranger; and the whole of that time he had smiled only twice: once when Matrena first had prepared supper for him, and once when the great gentleman had come to the house.

Simon was delighted with Michael as his workman. He no longer asked where he came from; his only fear was that Michael would some day leave him.

One day they were all sitting at home. Wife Matrena was putting an iron pot on the stove, and the children were running along the benches and looking out of the windows. Simon was stitching at one window, and Michael was hammering the heel of a boot at the other. One of the little boys came along the bench up to Michael, leaned against his shoulder, and looked out of the window.

"Look, Uncle Michael! A lady is coming with her children to our house, and one of the little girls is lame."

As soon as the boys said this, Michael threw down his work, turned to the window and looked out into the road.

Simon was amazed. Michael had not once looked into the road before, but now he had rushed to the window and was looking at something or other. Simon also looked out of the window, and he saw a lady coming straight towards his door; her clothing was elegant, and by the hand she led two little girls in furs, with kerchiefs round their heads. The children were as like as two peas. It was impossible to tell one from the other, only one of them was lame in one foot, and limped as she walked. The lady went up the stairs to the passage, fumbled at the door, groped for the latch, and opened the door, She pushed her two little children on before her, and entered the house.

"Good health, my master!"

"Pray come in. What can we do for you?"

The lady sat down on a chair; the children, shy,

pressed close to her knees. The good people looked on and wondered.

"Look, now," said the lady, "will you sew me leather shoes for the children against the spring?"

"I guess we can do that. We don't as a rule make little shoes for children, but we can do so, of course. You can have them welded or one-piece uppers, and linen lined. My Michael here is a master at his trade.

Simon glanced towards Michael, and saw he had thrown down his work, and was gazing at the children. He couldn't take his eyes from them.

Simon was amazed at Michael. It is true they were nice children -- black-eyed, plump-cheeked, rosy-faced -and their little furs and frocks were also very nice; but still Simon could not understand why Michael should look at them as if he recognized them from before.

Simon was amazed, but he began to talk to the

lady, and settled about the work to be done. They arranged it, and he got ready to take measurements. Then the lady took the lame little girl on her lap, and said:

"Take the measurements from this little one. Make one shoe for her left foot, and three from the measurements of the right foot. Both girls have the same shape of foot -- as like as two peas. They are twins."

Simon took the tiny measurements and said to the lame little girl:

"How did this happen to you? Such a nice little girl as you are too! Were you born with it?"

"No," said the lady, "her mother did it."

Matrena then drew near. She wanted to know who the woman was, and all about the twins. "Then you are not their mother?" she asked. "I am not their mother, nor indeed any relation. They were quite strangers to me, but I adopted them."

"They are not your children, eh? Yet you seem

very fond of them?"

"Why should I not be fond of them? I have fed them both from my breast. I had a child of my own, but God took him; yet I couldn't love my own child more than I love these." "Whose children then are they?"

\*          \*          \*

The woman began to speak, and this is what she said:

"It is now six years ago," said she, "since the parents of these orphans both died in one week. The father died on the Tuesday, and they buried the mother on the Saturday. These poor little things were born three days after their father died, and their mother did not live out the day of their birth. My husband and I lived at that time in the village. We were their neighbors; we dwelt side by side. The father of these children was a solitary man; he worked as a woodcutter. One day they were felling a tree, and it fell right upon him; all his insides were crushed. Scarcely had they brought him home than he gave up his soul to God; and his wife the same week bore these two little children. There was nothing in that house but poverty and loneliness. The poor mother was quite alone there; there was neither a nurse nor a midwife. Alone she bore them, and alone she died.

"I went in the morning to look after my neighbor. By the time I came to the hut, the poor thing was already cold.

In her agony, she had rolled upon this little girl - she had rolled upon this little girl, I say, and broken her leg. The people came together. They washed and tidied the body; they made a grave and buried her. They were all good people. The children remained all alone. What was to be done with them? I was the only woman of them all just then who had a suckling. I had been nourishing my dear little boy for eight weeks. I took the twin babies to my own house for the meantime. The farmers came together; they thought and thought what to do with the children, and they said to me: 'Maria, keep the children for a time at your house, and give us time to think the matter over.'

At first I gave my breast only to the well child, and the one that had been injured I did not feed at all. I didn't expect her to live. But soon I thought to myself, 'How can you bear to see this little angel face pining away?' So I began to give it suck also. I fed my own and these two as well -- three at my breast I fed. I was young and strong, and I had good food. God gave me an abundance of milk. I used to feed two at a time, while the third waited -- then I would remove one and feed the third. God helped me to nourish all three, but in the second year I buried my own child. And God gave me no more children, although we began to prosper. We live now at the mill with the grain-dealer; my husband gets good pay and our life is pleasant. But we have no children of our own. How could I bear to live alone, if it were not for these children? And how dear they are to me! Without them I would be a candle without wax."

With one hand the lady pressed the lame little

girl to her side, and with the other she wiped the tears from her cheeks.

"It is plain," said Matrena, "that the proverb is true which says, 'We can live without father and mother, but we cannot live without God.'"

So they went on talking, and the woman rose to go. As the shoemaker conducted her out, the room became bright with light. They looked at Michael, he was sitting with his hands folded on his knees, he looked upwards with a smile, and there was light all about him.

\*           \*           \*

Simon went up to him. "What is it, Michael?" said he.

Michael stood up and put down his work. Then he took off his apron, bowed to the shoemaker and his wife, and said: "Farewell, my host and hostess. God has forgiven me; you must forgive me too."

And the shoemaker and his wife saw that the radiance came from Michael. So Simon stood up and bowed low to Michael, and said to him:

"I see, Michael, that you are no mere man, and I am not able to keep you, nor am I able to ask you any question. Tell me, nevertheless, this one thing -- why, when I found you and brought you to my home, were you so sad; and why, when my Matrena gave you food that first night, did you smile, and from then on brighten up? Then again, when the great gentleman ordered the boots, you smiled a second time; and from that time forth you became brighter still. Now, when the lady brought these children for their shoes, you smiled a third time, and grew exceedingly bright. Tell me now, Michael, whence is this light, and why did you smile these three times?"

And Michael said: "Light comes forth from me, because although I was punished, God has now forgiven me. I smiled three times because God sent me to learn three divine lessons. Now I have learned them. I learned the first divine lesson when your wife had compassion on me, and then I smiled the first time. I learned the second divine lesson when the great man ordered his boots, and so I smiled the second time; and just now, when I saw the children, I learned the third divine lesson, and I smiled for the third time."

Simon said: "Tell me now, Michael, why did God punish you, and what are those divine lessons -- so that I too may learn them?"

And Michael answered: "God punished me because I was not obedient. I was an angel in Heaven, and God sent me to take away the soul of a woman. I flew down to the earth, and saw there a woman who lay sick. She had just given birth to little twin girls; they moved weakly beside their mother, and she was too weak to be able to put them to her breast. The woman saw me, and understood that God had sent me for her soul. She burst into tears, and said: 'Angel of God! They have only just buried my husband; he was struck dead by a tree of the forest. I have neither sister, nor aunt, nor grandmother, no one at all to bring up my poor orphans. Do not take away my poor, wretched soul, let me but feed and nourish my little children till they can stand upon their feet. How can the children live to grow up with neither a father nor mother?' And I listened to the mother. I laid one child on her breast, I put the other child in her arms, and I ascended to the Lord in Heaven. I flew up to the Lord, and said to him: 'I cannot take the soul away from that poor mother. The father was killed by a tree, the mother has borne twins, and she prayed me not to take the soul out of her, and said "Let me but feed and nourish my little children till they can stand upon their feet. How can the children live to grow up with neither father nor mother?" And so I did not take away the soul of the poor mother.' Then God said, 'Go and fetch hither the soul of the mother, and learn three lessons. Thou shalt learn What is given to men, *What is not given to men*, and *What men live by*. When thou hast learnt these things, thou shalt return to heaven.' And I flew back again upon the earth, and took away the soul of the woman. The little ones fell from her breast. The dead body fell back upon the bed, pressed upon one of the little children, and broke her leg. I rose above the village; I was carrying the soul to God. Then a blast of cold wind caught me, my wings dropped down and fell off, and the soul went alone to God; but I fell to the earth by the wayside."

*         *         *

And Simon and Matrena understood who it was they had clothed and fed, and who had lived with them, and so they wept for fear and joy. Then the Angel said:

"I was alone in the field and naked. Never had I known before the needs of man; never before had I known hunger and cold, and what it is to be a man. I grew more and more hungry; I was freezing, and I knew not what to do. I looked about me; I saw in the field a shrine made for God; I went to this shrine of God; I wanted to shelter myself in it. But the shrine was locked with bar and bolt; there was no getting into it. I sat me down by the shrine to be sheltered from the wind. Evening drew on. My hunger grew; I was freezing, and racked with pain. All at once I heard a man coming along. He was carrying boots, and talking to himself. It was the first time I had seen a human face while feeling what it was like to be a man. I had a horror of this face, and turned away from it. And I heard how this man was talking to himself, and how he asked himself how he was to protect his body against the cold of winter and provide for his wife and children. And I thought to myself, 'Here am I perishing from cold and hunger; but this man can never help me because he can only think of how he is to clothe himself against the winter and provide his family with bread.' The man saw me and was troubled. Then a still greater fear seized him, and he hurried by. I was in despair. Suddenly I heard the man coming back. I looked and could not recognize 131 the man I had seen before. Then there had been death in his face, but now he had suddenly become a living soul, and in his face I recognized God. He came to me, clothed me, took me with him, and led me to his house. I entered his house. His wife came out to meet us and began to speak. The woman was even more dreadful than her husband had been. The spirit of death came from her mouth, and I could not breathe in the deathly air around her. She wished to drive me forth into the cold, and I knew that if she drove me forth, she would die. Then all at once her husband reminded her of God, and a great change suddenly came over the woman. And when she gave me some supper she looked at me, and I looked at her, and Death was no longer upon her --she was a living soul, and I recognized God in her.

"And I remembered the first lesson of God: 'Thou shalt learn *What is given to men.*' Then I knew that love has been given to men, to dwell in their hearts. And I rejoiced that God had begun to reveal to me what He had promised, and I smiled for the first time; but I was not yet able to understand everything. I did not understand what is not given to men, nor what men live by."

"I began to live with you, and a year went by. And the man came and ordered boots -- boots that would last a year and neither loosen nor split. And I looked at him, and suddenly I saw behind him my companion, the Angel of Death. No one but me saw this Angel, but I knew him; and I knew also that before the sun went down he would take away the soul of the rich man. I thought to myself, 'This man makes plans for a year, and he knows not that he will die before tonight'; and I remembered the second lesson of God: "Thou shalt learn *What is not given to men*." What mankind was given I knew already. Now I knew what is not given to mankind. It is not given to men to know their own needs. And I smiled the second time. And I rejoiced that I had seen my companion Angel, and that God had revealed to me the second lesson."

"But I was not yet able to understand everything. I was not able to understand yet what men live by; and I lived on and waited until God should reveal the last lesson to me. Then in the sixth year came the woman with the twin children, and I knew the children, and I knew that they had been kept alive. I knew it, and I thought, 'The mother begged me to spare her to save her children, and I believed the mother; I thought that without father or mother it was impossible for children to live; and lo! a strange woman has nourished them and brought them up. And when the woman wept with joy over another's children, I saw in her the living God, and knew what men live by; and I knew that God had revealed the last lesson to me, and had forgiven me, and I smiled for the third time."

*　　　　　　*　　　　　　*

And the clothes fell from the body of the Angel, and he was clothed with light so that no eye could bear to look upon him, and he began to speak more terribly, as if his voice did not come from him, but from Heaven. And the Angel said:

"I learnt that man does not live by care of himself, but by love for others. It was not given the mother to know what was needful for the life of her children; it was not given to the rich man to know what was needful for himself; and it is not given to any man to know whether by the evening he will want boots for his living body or slippers for his corpse. When I came to earth as a man, I lived not by care for myself, but by the love that was in the heart of a passer-by, and his wife, and because they were kind and merciful to me. The orphans lived not by any care they had for themselves; they lived through the love that was in the heart of a stranger, a woman who was kind and merciful to them. And all men live, not by reason of any care they have for themselves, but by the love for them that is in other people."

"I knew before that God gives life to men, and desires them to live; but now I know far more. I know that God does not desire men to live apart from each other, and therefore has not revealed to them what is needful for each of them to live by himself. He wishes them to live together united, and therefore has revealed to them that they are needful to each other's happiness."

"I know now that people only *seem* to live when they care only for themselves, and that it is by love for others that they really live. He who has Love has God in him, and is in God -- because God *is* Love."

And the Angel sang the glory of God, that the house trembled at his voice, and the roof parted asunder, and a pillar of fire shot up from earth to Heaven. Simon and his wife fell down with their faces to the ground; and wings burst forth from the Angel's shoulders, and he rose into Heaven.

And when Simon raised his eyes again, the house stood there as before, and in the house there was no one but his own dear family.

# BIBLIOGRAPHY

Below are a few biographical and critical studies of Tolstoy's life and works that may serve the further interests of readers of this publication.

Bulgakov, Valentin. The Last Year of Leo Tolstoy, translated by Ann Dunnigan. New York: The Dial Press, 1971.

Chertkoff, Vladimir. The Last Days of Tolstoy, translated by Natalie A. Duddington, London: William Heinemann, 1922.

Christian R. F. Tolstoy's Letters. New York: Charles Scribner's Sons, 1978.

Crosby, Ernest. Tolstoy and His Message. London: The Simple Life Press, 4 Water Lane, London, E. C., 1903.

Derrick, Leon. Tolstoy, His Life and Work. London: Routledge, 1944.

Dole Nathan. The Life of Count Tolstoy. New York: Thomas Y. Crowell Co., New York, 1911.

Maude, Aylmer. The Life of Tolstoy. 2 Vols. Tolstoy Centenary Edition. London: Oxford, 1929-30.

Maude, Aylmer. Tolstoy on Art. Boston: Small, Maynard and Co., 1924.

Nazaroff, A. I. The Inconstant Genius. New York: Stokes, 1929.

Rolland, Romain. The Life of Tolstoy, translated by Bernard Miall. New York: Dutton, 1911.

Simmons, Ernest J. Leo Tolstoy. Boston: Little, Brown and Company, 1946.

Simmons, Ernest J. Introduction to Tolstoy's Writings. Chicago: University of Chicago Press, 1968.

Steiner, E. A. Tolstoy, The Man and His Message. New York: F. H. Revell, 1908.

Sukhotin-Tolstoy, Tatiana. The Tolstoy Home, translated by Natalie A. Diddington, London: William Heinemann, 1922.

Tolstoy, Alexandra. Tolstoy. A Life of My Father, translated by E. R. Hapgood, New York: Harper, 1953.

Tolstoy, Ilya. Tolstoy, My Father, translated by Ann Dunnigan. Chicago: Cowles Book Company, Inc., 1971.

Troyat, Henri. Tolstoy. New York: Dell Publishing Co., Inc., 1969.

Zweig, Stefan. The Living Thoughts of Tolstoy. New York: Longmans, Green and Co., 1939.

Lucas, Victor. Tolstoy in London. London: Evans Brothers Limited, 1979.

# Tolstoy Museum

Tourists who visit Russia can go to the museum-estate Yasnaya Polyana, the place where the great writer was born, spent almost all of his life and was buried. This museum-estate is located about 120 miles south of Moscow, close to the historical town of Tula. In Moscow, there are two museums: the Tolstoy House Museum and State Tolstoy Museum.

Address of State Museum, Yasnaya Polyana:
Russia, 301214, Tula region, Shekenskiy County,
Yasnaya Polyana.
Tel: (0872) 38-67-09
E-mail:<tour@yaspol.tula.su>

Address of L.N. Tolstoy State Museum: Prechistinka street, 11. Moscow, Russia.
Tel: (7495)202-21-90

Address of L.N. Tolstoy House Museum: Leo Tolstoy street, 21. Moscow, Russia.
Tel: (7495)951-64-40

# Illustrations

| | |
|---|---|
| Leo Tolstoy with daughter Alexandra | v |
| Tolstoy, Moscow 1868 | vi |
| Tolstoy, 1854. The happiest time of his life | xii |
| Tolstoy at the University, 1847 | 48 |
| Tolstoy in 1856 | 49 |
| Sophia Behrs the year before her marriage to Tolstoy | 50 |
| Tolstoy at the time of his marriage, October 5, 1862 | 51 |
| Sisters Sofia Tolstoy and Tatyana Behrs, 1862 | 52 |
| Tolstoy in 1876 | 53 |
| Tolstoy in 1881 | 54 |
| Countess Sophie Andreyvna Tolstoy in 1881 | 55 |
| Tolstoy in 1885 | 56 |
| Tolstoy in 1887 | 57 |
| M.K. Gandhi's letter to Tolstoy | 58 |
| Tolstoy in his Library | 59 |
| Tolstoy in his study | 60 |
| A tea party | 61 |

| | |
|---|---|
| Tolstoy in 1892 | 62 |
| Tolstoy in 1908 | 63 |
| Tolstoy on a walk | 64 |
| Tolstoy returning from bathing | 65 |
| Tolstoy is reading in his family circle | 66 |
| Tolstoy and his wife Sofia in 1910 | 67 |
| Tolstoy and his daughter Alexandra | 68 |
| Tolstoy in 1910 | 69 |
| Tolstoy, one of his last photographs | 70 |
| A phonograph presented to Leo Tolstoy by Thomas Edison, 1910 | 71 |
| Tolstoy in his death bed | 72 |
| Funeral procession for Tolstoy | 73 |
| The grave of Tolstoy | 74 |
| Michael Levin, winter 1974, Yasnaya Polyana | 75 |
| A picturesque corner of Yasnaya Polyana | 76 |
| Michael Levin in front of the Museum of Leo Tolstoy Moscow, October 1993 | 77 |
| A view of Yasnaya Polyana in summer | 78 |
| A view of Yasnaya Polyana in winter | 79 |
| The Chapel of St. Mark's college in Chelsea in London | 80 |

Author in October, 1993 researching Tolstoy's
   trip to London      81

Michael Levin at the funeral of
   Alexandra Tolstoy October 1st, 1979      114

Tatiana Schaufuss, lifelong friend
   of Alexandra Tolstoy      115

Tatiana Schaufuss      116

Alexandra Tolstoy in her coffin      117

Coffin of Alexandra is closed      118

The gravesite is closed (who is this girl?)      119

The cross on the grave of Alexandra Tolstoy      120

Additional Photos      129

This book is a valuable addition to Tolstoy scholarship. Perhaps the most significant achievment of the book is its analysis of Tolstoy's thought and philosophy. It successfully treads a fine line between a memoir and a work of literary, historical and sociological criticism. The memories of Tolstoy's daughter, Alexandre Lvovna Tolstoy, in her later days at Valley Cottage, the circumstances of which cannot be known to everyone, add a very personal note.

M. Richards
London, England

This book brought back many memories of stories my grandmother use to tell. Many of the quotes in the book I will be able to use in my sermons.

Evelyn Finney
Gilroy, California
United States of America

# To the Publishers of "A Signature on a Portrait:"

I am currently a freshman at the University of Southern California. In the schoool's library, I rummaged trough all the books written by and about Leo Tolstoy. I came across your insightful book on the literary legend. As I read your book, I learned many touching and influential dimensions to Leo Tolstoy. To me, Tolstoy's beauty lies in his pure and spiritual teachings. I am enamored with the life he led, the power of his works, and the beauty of his philosophies. I stand in both awe and exhilaration at all he said, did and wrote. Thus, I ask you to please mail me a copy of your book titled, "A Signature on a Portrait - Highlights of Tolstoy's Thoughts." This would be greatly appreciated. I hope to hear from you soon. Thank you.

Lisa Ho Tong
Los Angeles, California

Precisely found form – limited formation of the anthology from religious philosophical works of L.N. Tolstoy, fragments of memory recollections, analysis of him and your personal perception of Tolstoy's teaching allows actuality of his creation and ethical studies in present day life.

Joyfully to understand, that in our difficult time, when immorality and Mammon are celebrated, "live trembling threads" of understanding and spiritual closeness, connecting Leo Tolstoy with people now living in different corners of the Planet Earth.

Pages of the book, narrating your friendship and relationship with Alexandra Lvovna Tolstoy, with her life embodying the ethics of her great father and most of all action of kindness and love which is so very dear to us.


Pancheva G.N..

Manager of the Book Fund of Tolstoy Museum, in Yasnaya Polyana, Tula, Russia.

# By the same Author

Last Spring in Bakuriani

First Love

Kentucky Derby 82 or "Gato del Sol"

Reward

Visit Tolstoy's places in London

Comnabula

Charly

The Man with Briefcase

The Miner and his pigeons

Some reminiscences and reflections

First Spring streams or Children joy

Chepemnet

Mr Polonskiy

Drum Boogie

Jacob

Meeting old friend in New World

"Hunting row" subway station

The end in "Paradise".